Deadly
Harvest

Deadly

John M. Kingsbury

Harvest

A Guide to Common Poisonous Plants

Holt, Rinehart and Winston
New York

Designer: Ernst Reichl
ISBN: 0–03–091479–5
Printed in the United States of America

10 9 8 7 6 5 4 3 2

Dedicated to the memory of

Walter Conrad Muenscher

Introduction

Despite the headlong increase in our factual knowledge and the geometric proliferation of scientific specialties, few persons, professional or amateur, know much about poisonous plants. Surprisingly, perhaps, we are still largely in the Dark Ages as regards this aspect of the natural world.

Thousands of persons each year receive medical attention after incidents involving plants and hundreds of thousands of animals, wild and domestic, are poisoned annually. Yet we do not even record accurately the incidence of poisoning and we cannot assess reliably the danger to man or animals from any plant, or from all plants.

Rachael Carson alerted the general population and reminded scientific specialists of what man is capable of doing to the environment he shares with other living species. In the ensuing spirited debate, no one has pointed to the danger already present in the natural world, before man began to change it. Great financial resources have been mustered to conduct research into the total effect of man-made poisons but research directed toward finding out more about the plants themselves that kill has been minor, haphazard, intermittent and precariously supported.

Anyone who can read and follow simple printed directions can go into a pharmacy and utilize its services with great safety although in fewer places is there a larger collection of poisons. On the other hand, you can go into almost any supermarket and obtain an attractive product, with no warning attached, that is lethal if eaten in even a small amount. Packets of castor-bean seeds are sold at

flower-seed displays in supermarkets across the country. These, poin-
settias, oleander, rosary pea, and many other dangerous plants, commonly available, do not bear warning labels, yet most persons are
unaware of their potentially lethal nature.

Why has there been so little research in the toxicology of poisonous plants, especially when such great quantities of federal, state,
and private funds are currently directed into science and medicine?
The compartmentalization of science, in my opinion, is mainly responsible. Few natural scientists competently span the spectrum
from molecule to plant (or in other words from poison to the agent
that produces it). Few, in their academic upbringing and research
capacities, bridge the artificial chasm between plant and animal,
though the toxicology of plants cannot be adequately studied without examining both the poisoned and the poisoner. Perhaps fewer
still tie together the purely academic and the entirely practical,
yet it is largely through attempts to get practical answers to problems of poisoning that poisoning is investigated and identified. The
most eminent research specialist is often no better informed in areas
beyond his specialty than the average educated man.

The full investigation of poisoning from a plant first requires
mustering a team of specialists, which may include a physician or
veterinarian, to determine the incidence of poisoning in the animal
or human population, and to effectuate treatment and control; a
pathologist, to find, describe, and evaluate the signs of disease; an
animal physiologist or toxicologist, to determine the basic bodily
function deranged and how it is upset; a taxonomic botanist, to
identify with certainty the species of plant; a biochemist or organic
chemist, to isolate and identify the toxic compound; a clinician, to
direct experiments and follow the course of poisoning in experimental cases; a plant physiologist, to examine factors influencing
production of the toxic compound in the plant; an agronomist, to
analyze the effects of fertilization, herbicides, insecticides, and other
cultural practices in the case of crop plants displaying toxicity; a
nutritionist, to examine the degree to which nutritional stress in
the subject determines the form and severity of poisoning; and an
animal husbandman, to examine practices of management that
predispose to poisoning in domestic animals (often the most significant feature in such a case).

Probably all these competencies have never been gathered to investigate a specific problem; only rarely have even just two of them
combined in such an investigation. The physician or veterinarian

who encounters poisoning from plants usually feels that his training leaves him at a blank wall when it comes to the botanical aspects of a diagnosis of plant poisoning. Frequently he does not know
how to proceed to obtain outside help even if he wants to. The potential link between the hospital or veterinary practice and a research investigation is broken before it is even established.

Another significant problem arises from the current massive federal research grant which is awarded only after critical review by
evaluating panels composed of subject-matter specialists. In the
larger research institutions, whether state or private university or
independent group, few if any large-scale investigations are undertaken without federal support through the National Science
Foundation, the National Institutes of Health, the Department of
Defense, or similar agencies. The course of research is thus directly
influenced by the decisions of the evaluating panels, and unless
the compositions of such panels is broad, broadly conceived research
projects may suffer.

In this book, I have attempted to mount a small campaign for better understanding of poisonous plants; to create a better-informed
public so that poisonings may occur with less frequency despite the
move to suburbia; to make the dimensions of the problem more
generally known; to encourage the undertaking of significant research.

Scientists writing for the general reader have difficulty in group-
ing the specifics of the myriad fact with which they work into readily
comprehensible, yet, at the same time, scientifically valid generality.
So many exceptions exist to plague the essence of each generality.
To state the generality unequivocally is to ignore the exceptions.
Yet, when dealing with poisonous plants, to ignore the exceptions
is especially dangerous. My own technical volume,[1] written primarily for physicians and veterinarians, appropriately covers and documents the specifics, for those who require them.

I have attempted here to pick out unusually interesting and particularly instructive stories about the poisonous nature of plants.
Furthermore, and of greatest importance, I have included all those
plants that, on the present record, seem most likely to get human
beings into trouble. While it is impossible to describe each of these
plants so that anyone may recognize them beyond question, I hope
the descriptive comments, and especially the illustrations, will en-

[1] John M. Kingsbury, *Poisonous Plants of the United States and Canada.*
Prentice-Hall, Inc., Englewood Cliffs, New Jersey, 1964.

able the reader to spot the dangerous plants in his local vegetation, and will tell him what to do about them.

I should like to thank Elfriede Abbe and Louise G. Kingsbury, my wife, for their kindness in allowing me to use their lovely drawings in this book.

John M. Kingsbury

Scraggy Neck
Cataumet, Massachusetts

Contents

1. Introducing Poisonous Plants, 15

2. History, 30

3. Where Is Toxicity?, 40

4. How Plants Are Toxic, 75

5. Plants Everyone Should Recognize As Dangerous 109

6. What To Do About Poisonous Plants, 120

   Index, 125

Deadly
Harvest

1
Introducing Poisonous Plants

What is a poisonous plant?

About 300,000 species of plants exist on our earth. Records indicate that somewhat more than 700 of these have caused loss of life or serious illness in man or animals in this hemisphere; and many more, certainly, are not yet known to be poisonous. For example, even though wisteria is common in many parts of the country and has been for years, we learned only recently that wisteria is poisonous. Children who eat the seeds or pods of wisteria suffer serious gastrointestinal disturbances and may require hospitalization and drastic treatment. When this was brought generally to the attention of physicians as a poisonous plant, there came to light more than a score of cases of poisoning in children which previously had not been put on public record. Fortunately no fatalities have as yet occurred.

Defining a poisonous plant as one which has produced serious illness or loss of life in man or animal is perhaps most practical, but this leaves out those poisonous plants with no record of toxicity as yet. We think of a poisonous plant as one containing a specific substance, often still unidentified, which produces a deleterious reaction in the body of man or animals when taken in small or moderate amount.

Several diseases associated with plants cannot be considered poisonings. Examples include illness resulting from the lack of a nutritionally necessary factor, or illness from overindulgence, as in the case of livestock which become severely ill after gorging themselves on grain.

Moreover, a host of plants cause allergenic reactions. Such plants contain substances called allergens to which the human body can react by becoming abnormally sensitive. Two of the most common kinds of allergies are the "hay fever" reactions to pollens in the air and the dermatitic (skin rashes, etc.) reactions to contact with certain plants. Sensitivity to a particular plant varies among individuals as does the number of plants to which one person may be unusually sensitive. Almost any plant may produce hay fever or skin rash in an individual, but a small number of plants produce dermatitis in many persons. Though the physician does not classify an allergenic reaction, no matter how severe, as poisoning, most laymen think first of poison ivy when asked to name a poisonous plant.

Poison ivy, poison oak, and poison sumac are closely related and all contain a substance which is chemically similar to lacquer. In fact lacquer itself is obtained from another member of the same group of plants and produces in many persons a reaction similar to that caused by poison ivy. Perhaps you know someone who breaks out in a rash after handling Japanese lacquerware. Cashew, also, is closely related to poison ivy and shells of cashew nuts contain a lacquerlike molecule which may cause dermatitis.

Like lacquer, the allergen molecule of poison ivy remains in the dead plant and on clothing, decreasing little in potency for years unless removed by washing. The sensitizing resin is contained in all parts of the plant, but is not present on the surface until the plant has been bruised. This doesn't help sensitized persons much, however, because severe winds or a dog brushing through the plant are enough to bring the allergen to the surface of leaves. Poison-ivy resin is nonvolatile and cannot produce dermatitis unless a person actually contacts the active compound, yet many believe they have gotten poison ivy simply by going near a plant. In such cases, the explanation usually lies in the fact that the person contacted the

Wisteria

Poison ivy
With leaflet variation

*Left: redrawn from Cornell
Ext. Bull. 191, 1930*

plant without knowing it, by touching an exposed root or leafless branch. Then, too, the allergen may have been carried to the person on particles of carbon in smoke, or by pets, or on clothing or tools.

Once contacted, the poisonous substance remains on the skin tenaciously. It can be removed by thorough washing with strong soap, but to be effective, washing must be performed within five or ten minutes after contact. Otherwise the skin reaction will already have taken place, even though a rash doesn't appear for some hours. The fluid present in the blisters of poison-ivy rash cannot produce the reaction in other persons or on other places on the same person. The allergen, however, can be spread by scratching or in the course of treating the disease unless it has first been removed by washing or by flaking of skin.

Poison-ivy dermatitis is what is called a self-limiting disease. Many and varied treatments are suggested by persons who sincerely believe that they work, but in repeated controlled tests by physicians it has been established conclusively that in the ordinary case no real benefit, except perhaps psychological, is obtained from most familiar remedies, either in speeding the course of disease or in reducing its severity. Certain ointments may relieve itching. This is important because scratching makes the irritation more severe, promotes infection, and may spread the allergen to other areas of skin. Whatever relieves itching in individual cases is best to use. In severe cases a physician may use cortisone to reduce symptoms.

Like most allergies, sensitivity to poison ivy disappears slowly in the absence of additional exposures. The rate at which it disappears varies as greatly among individuals as does the ease with which persons become sensitized in the first place. Probably no one is absolutely immune to sensitization. Most persons notice that they are less sensitive after two or three years of nonexposure, but for many people decades pass before sensitivity is considerably reduced. Each exposure to poison ivy increases sensitivity in proportion to the degree of exposure. Some areas of skin may become more sensitive than others because of repeated contact.

Since the allergen is the same among poison ivy, poison oak, and poison sumac, exposure to one sensitizes to all. The best way to cope with these plants is to learn to recognize them and stay away from them. People who have occupations which make this impossible should seek artificial desensitization from a physician. This procedure usually first involves determining, by skin tests, the initial degree of sensitivity, and administering, by injection or orally, small but increasing concentrations of a compound derived from or related to the allergen. This series of treatments slowly builds up the subject's resistance to the natural allergen, though it may need to be repeated from year to year.

Unfortunately, poison ivy and poison oak are not easily recognized and poison sumac is even more difficult to avoid in its natural brushy or swampy habitat.

Poison ivy and poison oak are extremely variable plants. They may occur as ground vines, climbing vines, or shrubs, and they are widely distributed in hedge rows, thickets, woods, and along roadsides and the like throughout the country. The leaves, also, vary greatly in size, texture, and degree of incutting of the margin. Persons accustomed to recognizing these plants in one part of the country often do not recognize them at all elsewhere. It helps to remember that poison ivy is woody in older plants and that each

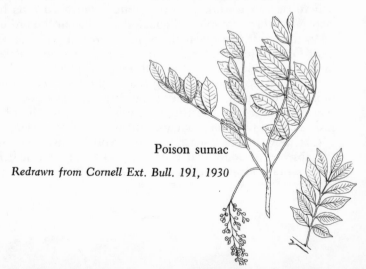

Poison sumac

Redrawn from Cornell Ext. Bull. 191, 1930

leaf is divided into three separate leaflets as illustrated in Figure 2. Fruiting plants bear a cluster of small white berries.

Poison sumac is a tall shrub or small tree. Each leaf is composed of 7 to 11 leaflets arranged oppositely along a conspicuously red central axis, with one leaflet at the tip (Figure 3). Each leaflet is bright green and without sharply pointed edges, an important factor which distinguishes poison sumac from its nonpoisonous relatives.

I have discussed poison ivy, poison oak, and poison sumac in some detail because they are thought of as poisonous plants by many persons and because they are frequent sources of human discomfort. But neither these allergenic plants or other dermatitis or hay-fever plants are poisonous in the strict sense of the term because true poisoning, unlike allergy, does not depend on a pre-existing sensitivity.

The differences between a plant-caused allergy and plant poisoning may be illustrated further by citing some examples of plants which produce a dermatitislike but nonallergenic reddening or burning of the skin. Leafy spurge, sun spurge, caper spurge, spotted spurge, snow-on-the-mountain, and other spurges contain sap acrid enough to burn the skin under certain conditions. The juice of snow-on-the-mountain has been used in place of an iron for branding cattle in Texas. The burn produced by the irritant properties of the sap of these plants is like that produced by an acid. Some parts of the body—the tissue about the eyes, for example—are more easily burned than others.

The manchineel tree, a small tropical tree, occasionally found south of Palm Beach and Fort Myers in Florida, caused a lot of trouble for the early settlers. People were temporarily and some-

Snow-on-the-mountain

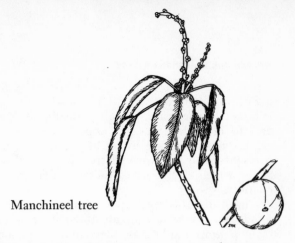

Manchineel tree

times permanently blinded when this tree's sap got into their eyes, as often happened to those using an ax on the tree. The manchineel tree is relatively rare now in Florida because the first inhabitants destroyed it wherever they found it.

In addition to the eyes, the tissues of the digestive tract are especially delicate and easily inflamed by caustic plant juices. Spurges actually cause more trouble by producing intense digestive discomfort or death in animals eating them than by producing skin burns in man. Severe digestive upset may take place in children who take a mouthful or two of such a plant. This is worth remembering because certain spurges are used as ornamental plants and, although less potent than some of the wild spurges, are more readily available to curious children. These include snow-on-the-mountain and cypress spurge, sometimes planted in outdoor gardens, crown of thorns, candelabra cactus, pencil tree, and the familiar poinsettia. All of these may produce severe gastric distress if eaten and poinsettia has been responsible for deaths among children.

Wild spurges are not easily recognized. They are weedy plants found widely across the United States. The sap is white, milky, and usually quite obvious as it wells from the broken surface of a stem. (Other plants which are not dangerous, such as common dandelion, may also have milky sap.) Flowering spurges may be easily recognized by the basic construction of the "flower," which is not a flower at all, but a compound structure consisting of a whorl of 4 to 5 petal-like, small, colored leaves surrounding a cluster of male flowers, each of which is but a single stamen. In the exact center is a single female flower composed of but one pistil. The petal-like leaves are usually yellow or yellow-green, but in most varieties of poinsettia they are bright red and almost as large as the regular green leaves.

Poinsettia

To be considered poisonous a plant must contain a specific poisonous substance, the poisonous principle. Sometimes the chemical identity of the substance is known, as in the case of the irritant substance in the spurges. More often it has not been identified chemically. The spurge irritant is considered a low-grade poisonous principle because it produces a nonspecific, general irritation or inflammation of the tissues it contacts (unless they are too tough or calloused).

Most poisons have specific effect in the chemistry or function of the body. Different poisons do different things and from prehistoric time, man has made medicinal use of particular active substances in plants. Compounds such as digitalis, morphine, belladonna, and a host of others are very familiar. They are highly active substances and, in relatively small amounts, produce the desired beneficial effect. In larger amounts they are poisons and the plants from which they are obtained have caused loss of life in animals and sometimes in man. An arbitrary line must be drawn to distinguish between the amount of a compound which is useful and that which is dangerous.

Many diseases are caused by bacteria. Others, such as athlete's foot, are caused by fungi. Both bacteria and fungi are classed as plants and, although both produce trouble in the human body, we usually don't think of them as poisonous. They are, instead, infectious. However, some fungi, such as certain mushrooms, are truly poisonous. An example of bacterial poisoning is the very serious illness, botulism, found in a certain type of food spoilage.

Infectious diseases are distinguished from poisonings by the fact that they are caused by bacteria and fungi which live within and at the expense of the sick individual. To combat infections, the physician directs his major effort toward killing or chasing out the infecting organisms without injuring the patient. Poisonings, on the other hand, do not require the presence of a living organism, but only of the poison which it has produced.

Poisons and Food

In recent years food-processing companies have discovered and put to use many additive compounds, such as calcium proprionate, to retard mold contamination of baked goods, or monsodium gluta-mate, to enhance flavor. Some people refer to such compounds as "chemicals" and disparage their use in foods as unnatural. This type of protest is carried to an extreme by those who insist not only that such unnatural "chemicals" not appear in the food they buy, but also that the grains or other plant products which go into the foods be grown without the aid of chemical fertilizers. They seem to believe that there is danger in eating foods produced by "unnatural" conditions. The fervor with which they defend these views always surprises me, for, at the same time, they usually ignore the real danger in many of the *natural* chemicals in plants they eat daily.

There are many examples. Cabbage, turnip, rutabaga, and many other members of the cabbage family contain a chemical—L-5-vinyl-thiooxazolidone—which encourages goiter by preventing the thyroid gland from using some of the iodine in a normal diet and thus inhibiting formation of the thyroid hormone. These plants have caused goiter to develop in animals in iodine-deficient areas and they could do the same in man if eaten in abnormally large amounts during a period of time in which the diet did not contain ample iodine.

Tomato and potato plants contain a molecule called solanine, which is violently toxic. It first causes irritation and injury of the digestive tract, and then, after being absorbed through the injured tissue into the blood stream, causes malfunctions in the nervous system. The vines of both of these plants have killed livestock on many occasions and potato tubers have killed man and animals.

The true fruit of the potato is a small green berry found among the above-ground branches. The berrylike fruits of the closely related common nightshades also contain solanine and are attractive to children, but fortunately, the ripe fruit contains the least solanine of any part of the plant.

The part of the potato which we eat is not the fruit but the tuber,

Black nightshade

actually a swollen portion of an underground stem, not root, into which the plant packs starch and other reserve food materials.

Solanine is always present in potato tubers to some degree, the normal content being about one tenth of the amount necessary to produce symptoms if a very large meal of potatoes were consumed at one time. But under some circumstances, as described below, solanine may be concentrated in potato tubers to a lethal level. Solanine is not distributed equally in the tuber, but tends to be concentrated in the layer next to the skin. Solanine accumulation is greatest in areas which are green, such as "sun-burned" spots on potatoes and in the sprouts. It is wise practice to peel away sun-burned spots before use and always to remove sprouts before cooking. Spoiled potatoes should be discarded because they may contain more solanine than normal. Boiling potatoes tends to leech out the solanine into the cooking water where it is much diluted and perhaps partially destroyed. The skins of baked potatoes are harmless when eaten in normal quantities.

Lima beans are another common food which may contain a poisonous compound. The "chemical" in this case is HCN, sometimes called hydrocyanic or prussic acid or cyanide. Lima beans grown in the United States have never been found to contain more than 0.01 per cent HCN and this is an entirely safe level. However, beans from tropical countries usually contain more HCN and frequently may be very toxic. Levels as high as 0.3 per cent have been detected, although beans containing more than 0.02 per cent are potentially dangerous to livestock if fed in large amount. After livestock deaths from imported beans, a law was passed in the United States which requires that all shipments of lima beans to be used as food or feed must be analyzed for cyanide. Beans with more than 0.01 per cent cyanide are rejected, while Canada prohibits importation of beans with more than 0.02 per cent.

Moderate or large amounts of cultivated onions in the daily diet of animals for a week or more provoke severe, and eventually fatal anemia. Though the poisonous component is unknown, there is no evidence suggesting that onions would be less toxic to human beings who consumed similar large quantities.

Nutritional experimentation with laboratory animals has shown that very large amounts of spinach in a diet which provided a low level of calcium prevented absorption of enough calcium to meet minimum needs and that death eventually followed. There is in spinach a relatively high level of soluble salts of oxalic acid, a compound present in small amounts in many plants. Oxalic acid combines with calcium to form an insoluble precipitate (calcium oxalate) which cannot be used by the body. Beet tops are similarly high in soluble salts of oxalic acid (more than 10 per cent by weight).

Perhaps the most surprising example of toxicity in a common food is that of the apple. Medical records include the case of a man who considered apple seeds a delicacy. He saved them whenever he ate an apple; and when he had collected a cupful of seeds, he sat down to eat them all at once. They killed him. The poisonous "chemical" in apple seeds is also HCN (prussic acid or cyanide). Most persons know that wild cherries, a very close relative of the apple, contain HCN and that the pits (seeds) of cultivated cherries, peach, apricot, and some varieties of almond, all closely related to the wild cherries, have especially high concentrations of HCN.

Learning the potential toxicity of certain common food plants should not prevent anyone from continuing to enjoy and profit from them in the diet. Small amounts of the poisonous compounds contained in them are absolutely harmless. Potatoes are the most dangerous, yet think what vast quantities of potatoes are eaten around the earth every day without poisoning anyone. Public health authorities of both state and federal governments constantly survey the wholesomeness of food products of all sorts. It is reassuring to know that highly skilled specialists are concerned for the public well-being and that foods are constantly under surveillance to prevent danger from unwholesome additive "chemicals" or from natural poisonous components.

In this day of increasingly complex technology the human population is confronted with more and more toxic compounds or dangerously flammable liquids which are used in hundreds of commercial products. For many years laws have been enforced which require warning notices on products containing the most toxic or dangerous of these compounds and the laws have recently been changed to make them even more inclusive. You may have noticed that some packages have been redesigned with cautions against potential toxicity even more clearly displayed than before. Not only has the number of compounds which must be so labeled been increased, but the laws now require that notices be in large type and in contrasting ink. There are severe penalties for failure to comply and offending products may be removed from the market. The intention of the laws has been to provide warnings only for those products which have caused poisoning or real hazard, or might reasonably be expected to do so. Many of the imposed standards are based on the results of tests for toxicity with laboratory animals under properly controlled and humane conditions.

Poisonous Plants

It is interesting to speculate how the labeling law might be applied to poisonous plants. Many house plants, such as poinsettia, are clearly dangerous and nowadays they are sold not only at florists but even in drugstores and food markets. As the labeling law becomes more effective in pointing out the dangerous commercial products which are carried in such outlets, the consumer is apt to rely increasingly on the presence of protective labeling and may therefore be less aware of the danger in such common "natural" but undesignated commodities as house plants.

Precatory bean, also called rosary pea and several other common names, is a plant to which the labeling law might well be applied. The tiny bean itself is among the most highly toxic of natural materials, organic or inorganic. Each bean is ovoid, about three eighths of an inch long, with a smooth, glossy scarlet and jet-black surface. The seed looks as though it had been painted with bright red enamel and then dipped in black gloss enamel so that about one third of the seed became coated with black. A single one of these small, attractive seeds has been enough to kill an adult human being. Its poison is unusual among plants. It is technically called a phytotoxin (a toxin produced by a plant) and is chemically related to the toxins produced by bacteria (the toxin of botulism, for example) and to snake venoms. The unadulterated poison, given by injection, in amounts as small as one-hundred-millionth per cent of the subject's weight, can cause death. This means that five one-hundredthousandths of a grain of the phytotoxin from precatory bean might kill a one-hundred-pound person if given by injection. Few compounds of any kind equal this degree of toxicity.

Why phytotoxins are so poisonous is not clear. It can be shown that, when mixed with blood, they cause red blood cells to clump together; but this reaction does not seem to be the basis of their extreme toxicity in the body itself. They may act as enzymes or organic catalysts, bringing about breakdown of some of the vital native proteins of which the body is composed. The phytotoxins call forth an antibody response in the reacting subject which fights the effects of the toxin. This response is a natural protective reaction of the body and has been put to use by physicians in counteracting the effects of certain bacterial toxins. Antibodies, artificially produced, are immediately given the patient to help him fight off the effects of the poisonous toxin as soon as the disease is suspected. Theoretically and experimentally the same can be done for phytotoxin poisonings, but since each toxin requires a specific antibody, and there is small demand for antibodies specific for phytotoxins, none are readily available.

Precatory beans grow in pods, not unlike pea pods, which are produced on vines. The precatory bean plant is a long-lived climbing vine native to tropical countries throughout the world. It was introduced into Florida and has become established as a wild plant in citrus groves, along fencerows, and similar locations in the central and southern part of the state. Its seeds are very attractive to children, and therefore of great danger. But even greater danger

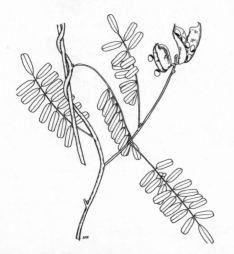

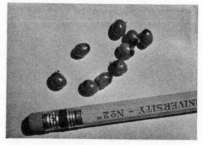

Precatory bean

Photo, Cornell Ext. Bull. 538, 1963

to human life comes from the use of precatory beans as jewelry which may thus be carried far from the area where the beans grow and where many persons know of their toxicity. Each year during my lectures on poisonous plants at Cornell University I ask my classes if anyone has seen a necklace, bracelet, or earrings in which precatory beans have been used. Nearly every year I find one or more students who either own such an object or know someone who has one. Rarely are they aware of the potential danger. Large numbers of such necklaces, bracelets, and other ornaments are produced in Puerto Rico, Mexico, and elsewhere and are imported into the United States despite governmental efforts to keep them out, or are brought back as souveniers by tourists and distributed widely.

Why do some plants contain poisonous substances?

It is difficult to explain the reason for toxicity in plants. The question itself usually grows out of Darwinian speculation in which it is assumed that characteristics of living species must exist because they provide that species some advantage in the competition for survival. Thus the conclusion might quickly be reached that plants which contain toxic compounds have a selective superiority over those which do not, because they kill the animals that might eat them. But this answer is too simple because to kill an animal the plant must be consumed and is thereby destroyed. In order to avoid them each animal must discover for itself which plants are poisonous or distasteful. Some poisonous plants are destroyed in this trial-and-error sampling process.

Nevertheless we have evidence that animals do learn to avoid poisonous plants effectively. In the experiences of many farmers and ranchers a pasture or range containing many poisonous plants had not actually caused trouble until animals from a different part of the country were placed in it. These new animals were poisoned. Sometimes mass loss of life has occurred. The conclusion is inescapable that animals familiar with the plants in the pasture had learned to discriminate between the toxic and the wholesome ones and to leave the former alone.

Animal discrimination of this sort undoubtedly spares many poisonous plants under pasture or range conditions. This increased survival value for the plants could explain evolution of toxicity if the conditions were to last long enough for significant evolution to take place (thousands or millions of years in most instances).

But fenced pastures and ranges and controlled animal harvesting are extremely recent and organized events, quite unlike those under which poisonous plants originally evolved. Wild animals are rarely killed by poisonous plants, since under natural conditions they feed selectively, much as man does, a little of this and a little of that. This habit means that they are much less likely to consume a dangerous amount of any one plant, and moreover that the time over which a given poisonous plant is consumed is lengthened. The latter is important because, if the plant is the kind which results in digestive disturbances, as the majority do, there will be time for the animal to feel its effects before a lethal amount has been consumed. Such types of poisoning tend to be self-correcting because, like yourself, animals with a severe stomach-ache stop eating. Certainly some wild animals have the capacity to learn which plants have frequently caused them this type of distress.

But even if we allow that some evolutionarily selective advantage may be gained by poisonous plants, it does not seem nearly sufficient to explain, for example, the fact that apple seeds contain HCN. The most reasonable general answer to the question, "Why do some plants contain poisonous substances?" is that in the course of evolution many poisonous compounds have developed more or less accidentally and, having neither strong selective advantage nor strong disadvantage for the species, are carried along from generation to generation as a genetically controlled characteristic.

Some practical matters

The medicines a physician employs exist in great number and variety. Both he and the pharmacist spend much time learning the specialized language and symbols by which prescriptions are written so that the pharmacist will supply *exactly* what the physician orders. The toxic compounds in plants also exist in great number and variety. In discussing or treating a case of plant poisoning it is as important to know exactly the plant involved as it is to specify medicines exactly, and for similar reasons. Common names are not exact. Not only does the common name for a particular species of plant often vary from place to place, but also the same common name is often used for several closely related species of plant. Names like buttercup and goldenrod refer to several different plants in each case. Names like sorrel and pigweed are used for different plants in different parts of the United States. Fortunately, botanists have been concerned with the identity of plant species since before the Middle Ages and have developed taxonomy, the science of identifying and naming plants, to a high degree the world over. Each species of plant has received a scientific name consisting of two words, the genus name followed by the species name. These names distinguish kinds of plants the same way individual persons are identified by given and family names. Scientific names are applied according to precise rules which are internationally followed. When a species is originally named, it is described in sufficient detail so that others may recognize it and distinguish it from all other species of plants. The description is published in Latin, a language not now in general use anywhere in the world and therefore not subject to the changes in language which take place slowly with popular usage.

We tend to think of poisonous plants first in relation to human beings, but, in reality, not nearly as much is known about poisoning of man as poisoning of animals. For one thing, the physician encounters cases of poisoning by plants only occasionally, while a veterinarian, especially one who deals with farm livestock, finds cases fairly frequently. Secondly, research into the toxic capacities of a poisonous plant or of compounds extracted from it is, for obvious reasons, conducted with animals rather than with man. Usually there is little fundamental difference between poisoning of animals and of man, but in some cases the difference is great and danger always accompanies trying to predict what will happen in the human organism from information which was derived from some other species of animal.

2
History

Knowledge of poisonous plants has accumulated gradually, each addition the result of experimental or circumstantial evidence, always subject to interpretation and further testing. We discard "facts" which rigorous tests prove incorrect. Our body of knowledge, then, is the product not only of what has been added, but also of what has subsequently been subtracted. Both processes are important in shaping the mass of our information and, of the "authority" from which the practicing physician or veterinarian must draw. We lack information about the toxic capacities of many plants (probably a majority of them) but even more dangerous, part of what we think we know will be proved incorrect; yet we cannot know how much is erroneous without detailed study and experimental testing. In such a setting not only is what has been said about a poisonous plant important but also who has said it.

Some rather surprising conclusions can be drawn from the sources of information about poisonous plants. In the rise of civilizations, tribes which lived by hunting preceded those dependent on agriculture. The poisonous properties of plants were put to practical use by primitive peoples before plants were used as crops. The word "toxic" comes from the ancient expression used originally to designate arrow poisons and is one of the oldest words in the language. The poisonous properties of indigenous plants were known to prehistoric tribes in many parts of the earth and some primitive peoples still employ plant poisons in hunting. The practical knowledge of plant poisons they have accumulated throughout history seems truly remarkable. Modern civilizations have not yet equaled all of their discoveries. For example, the drug reserpine on which our tranquilizers are based is obtained from the plant *Rauwolfia serpentina*, which has been used in India virtually since the beginning of history as a source of medicinal preparations. "Modern" scientific clinical knowledge of the active compound in it is less than ten years old.

The Greeks and the Romans collected medicinal information into compendia. Dioscorides, a follower of Socrates and Plato, concerned himself with the active properties of plants and other natural substances. He gathered a great amount of information into a compendium, written during the first century A.D., which he titled "Of Medicinal Matter." Like all writers of compendia who have followed him, Dioscorides had difficulty sorting out the valid from the supposed. Plants were not identified by exact scientific names until many centuries later, but botanists have devoted much detective work to learning the real identity of each plant which Dioscorides described. This has made his compendium useful to scholars of the present time, not only as an historical document, but also for the information it contains. An edition translated into English in the 1600's was supplemented with a list of plant names as we now use them, and has even been reprinted within the last few years.[1] Many of the plants we now know as toxic were also known as such to Dioscorides.

During the Middle Ages ignorance was compounded in most departments of knowledge, but this was not entirely the case for information concerning poisons, which were used with little hesitation in court intrigues, in ecclesiastical councils, and in promoting succession among the offspring of wealthy families. Such poisons were sold as "succession powders." Sometimes military campaigns were successful as the result of mass poisonings, for example, of the enemies' drinking water. Then, too, "Irritant substances were in some way or other applied to underclothing with the result that the victims died from an extensive dermatitis, or poisons were introduced into gloves and onto letters and books, with the hope that these poisons would eventually reach the mouth via the hands. The most popular way of poisoning was to add poison to the food or drink of the intended victim and frequently crockery, cutlery, and even toothpicks were contaminated with poisons. Victims were invited to meals and were given fruit or food which had come in contact with the poisoned side of the knife. Wholesale poisoning was effected by the contamination of wells and springs. Women rid themselves of men they deemed undesirable by applying poisons

[1] R. T. Gunther, editor, *The Greek Herbal of Dioscorides*. Hafner Publishing Company, New York, New York, 1959.

to their lips; such poisons were then introduced into the mouths of their victims during the act of kissing. Poisons were also mixed with oils and fats and rubbed into the skin and were even poured into the ears of sleeping victims, whilst the introduction of poisons into snuff was not uncommon. Jealousy, politics, and vengeance were at the bottom of all this ruthless poisoning of relatives, friends, and foes."[2]

Those who could employ poisons successfully often were able to name their own price for their services. The knowledge of poisons was conserved, protected, and even augmented. Secrets of the trade were jealously guarded. Extraneous ingredients were added to recipes so that it would be difficult for the uninitiated to identify the actual source of potency. As a result, by the fifteenth, sixteenth, and seventeenth centuries, a large amount of misinformation had deliberately been added to the records of poisons—misinformation which is sometimes easily recognized, but sometimes is not.

The reawakening began slowly. First efforts were aimed at re-examining information about the natural world which had been gathered during classical times and relating it to current experience. This presented particular problems when applied to plants because the flora of the Mediterranean countries which had concerned classical authors is different in many ways from the flora of Northern Europe and England. In some instances, classical authors were treated as though incapable of error. Many plants of Northern Europe and England were forced into identification with classical plants and active properties were incorrectly attributed to them.

Renaissance compendia dealing with plants were called herbals. The first printed herbal appeared around 1470 and this type of compendium continued to appear for about two hundred years. Most herbals were not very selective in content and only gradually did erroneous information and superstition give way to contemporary observation. As more information accumulated, herbals were succeeded by more specialized compendia and a split in content occurred, leading in one direction to books dealing with medicinal and useful properties of plants, and in the other, to floras, or catalogues of plants in a given geographic area. The poisonous nature of individual plants might be recorded in either type of publication.

Compilations limited to poisonous plants first appeared in Europe

[2] D. G. Steyn, *Toxicology of Plants in South Africa*. Central News Agency, Ltd., Johannesburg, South Africa, 1932.

around the turn of the eighteenth century. There was apparently a real effort to make information about them more widely known by publishing works in English, French, and German, instead of in Latin. Contents became more varied and did not depend solely on classical sources. Contemporary information came chiefly from observations of accidental cases of natural poisoning and results of overdoses of medicines (called "simples") derived from plants.

Most important, chance observation slowly began to give way to planned experimental investigation. The imaginative approaches of experimental pioneers such as Priestly, Lavoisier, Berthollet, and Scheele, and the new science of chemistry were strong influences on those interested in poisonous plants. Nearly half a dozen major books on poisonous plants were written before 1900. The number of species included increased greatly, despite the fact that each succeeding author eliminated plants he felt were poorly documented. In some cases, almost half the plants of the immediately preceding work were ignored. Many of the species added toward the end of the nineteenth century resulted from botanical exploration outside Europe.

In the United States, knowledge of poisonous plants has developed mostly from concern for the health of livestock and, therefore, through the development of scientific agriculture and veterinary medicine in this country. Joseph Priestly, discoverer of oxygen, came to America in 1794. He and men of Jefferson's administration, which began in 1801, did much to promote the cause of science in the young country. However, experimental agriculture did not fully develop for several decades. Difficulties in clearing the virgin lands and the Indian wars contributed to the delay, but most important was the fact that the farming population just did not believe in the value of science.

The Department of Agriculture was founded in 1862 and in the same year President Lincoln signed the Morrill bill which made federal resources in the form of land grants available to the states in support of agricultural education. But the establishment of professional training and standards in veterinary medicine did not come easily in this country. It was not until 1875 that people were being trained for experimental investigations of poisonous plants, and that the facilities to support them were becoming more available. The few reports concerning poisonous plants in the United States which appeared prior to 1875 drew heavily on European literature. But as our country was settled to the westward, and new lands were more intensively used, questions dealing with poisonous plants came in increasing number to the experimentalists in the Department of Agriculture and at the state experiment stations.

In 1884 a near-panic broke out in Kansas, which drew public attention to poisonous plants and initiated a formal investigation by the Department of Agriculture. Foot-and-mouth disease, one of the most dangerous diseases of cattle, was diagnosed in Kansas. If the diagnosis was correct, cattle, the primary economic resource of Kansas, would have to be quarantined. Several eminent veterinarians were immediately dispatched by the Army Veterinary Service, by several state governments, by the Canadian government and by the United States Department of Agriculture. Eventually the disease was correctly diagnosed as gangrenous ergotism and quarantine was unnecessary.

Ergotism is caused by ingestion of wheat, rye, and other grains which have been infested with growths of *Claviceps purpurea*, the ergot fungus. One stage in the life cycle of this fungus lives on the developing cereal grain and forms a hard, dark-colored mass, similar in shape but somewhat larger in size than the grain which it replaces in the fruiting head of the wheat or rye plant. One of the effects of its poisonous compounds is to cause constriction of the finer capillaries of the circulatory system. When this effect is strong enough, circulation is stopped in areas of lowest blood pressure farthest from the heart, as in the extremities. Tissues which are no longer supplied with blood in these locations die and usually break free or wear away. In cattle the hind feet are affected first and the hoofs may be sloughed off, so that the early stages resemble foot-and-mouth disease. Later, the front feet or legs, tips of the ears, tip of the tail and sometimes the tongue may become involved. The disease is called dry gangrene because the wounded surface does not bleed and there is no moist decay.

Outbreaks of ergotism in humans from contaminated grains reached epidemic proportions in certain European countries prior to 1800 and the disease was among the most dreaded. Occasional isolated outbreaks still occur in countries where control of cereal-grain purity is less than fully effective. Most cases in man are relatively mild and involve the joints of fingers or toes. In the United States, federal law prohibits use of grains containing more than 0.3 per cent of ergot by weight.

At the present time most ergotism in the United States is associated with ingestion of Dallis grass or Argentine bahia grass by

Fruiting head,
rye plant infested with ergot

cattle in the pastures of the South. These grasses sometimes become infested with heavy growths of *Claviceps paspali*, another species of ergot fungus, and ergot may be consumed in relatively large amounts. Under these circumstances the alkaloids act rapidly on the nervous system and, instead of slowly developing gangrene, the animal displays symptoms of nervous disorder, including convulsions. Convulsive erogtism can occur in human beings from ingestion of *Claviceps purpurea*, but it is very rare.

The year 1884 with its outbreak of ergotism in Kansas was the beginning of a period during which various problems concerning poisonous plants came under serious study in the United States and our literature on the subject began to increase importantly. Part of the increase may be traced to the influence of the Hatch Act (1887) which made federal funds available to the states in support of agricultural experimentation. Almost all of the investigation was associated with new farming lands and grazing ranges west of the Mississippi River. Poisonous plants of the West were initially emphasized in the investigations because the plants of eastern United States are generally identical with or similar to those of Europe, and it was possible for the settlers of the East to use information from European sources. The eastern part of our country had been settled and pragmatic agricultural practices had been established long before scientific agriculture came into being. Eastern farmers, having brought practical experience with them from the "old country," had soon learned what practices were best to avoid the poisoning of their livestock.

In the West, on the other hand, few of the plants were the same as those of Europe and no one knew their uses or their dangers. Frequent mass mortality of livestock occurred. Moreover the period when Western lands were first being settled and used corresponded roughly with the establishment of scientific agriculture in the United States. Soon after each state of the West was admitted to the Union, a state agricultural college and experiment station was established. Learning which were poisonous plants and what to do about them was one of the first problems these stations encountered.

Those nations of the world in which agricultural practice was well established before the advent of scientific experimentation still relied in large part on information about poisonous plants which had developed through chance happenings, influenced by human credulity and superstition. In countries settled later and in areas where the plants were different from those of Europe, new problems were dealt with scientifically as they arose. Thus, experimental investigations of poisonous plants have been more numerous and ambitious in South Africa, Australia, and western United States, for instance, than in France, India, and eastern United States. Pressures to investigate the nature of toxicity in plants recognized from antiquity as poisonous are much less than for those newly discovered as toxic. Only under special impetus is such an investigation initiated.

Compare, for example, what we know of the toxicity of daphne, an ornamental plant introduced from Europe, with our knowledge of the toxicity of loco, a plant of our Western range. Daphne is a relatively common ornamental shrub, usually 1 to 3 feet tall. Some daphnes may become naturalized among other shrubs in the Northeast. Small, showy, clustered flowers are produced along the bare stems in early spring and the somewhat laurellike new leaves come later. Each flower forms a small red berry (or other colors in some varieties and species) and the berries cluster along the woody stems among the leaf attachments.

Daphne berries are attractive to children. They contain a strongly irritant glycoside. Ingestion of only a few berries produces burning or ulceration in the digestive tract. Vomiting and diarrhea are usual and may contain blood. Death may result.

Daphne

Photo, Cornell Ext. Bull. 538, 1963

Surprisingly, we know little more about the toxicity of this plant than did Dioscorides who accurately described the symptoms and lesions. Since then, cases in human beings and animals have been reported from time to time and chemists have performed some extractions, looking for the toxic principle. But no one has learned much more than Dioscorides knew—especially concerning how much was toxic or what was an effective treatment. Even Orfila, who has been called "The Father of Toxicology," added little. In 1814 he described some experiments with dogs, using powdered daphne bark, which gave some idea of the toxicity of the bark to dogs but not necessarily of the berries to man. We have no idea of the relative toxicity of the several species of daphne, of variation in toxicity with season, or whether the plant is equally toxic under different growing conditions or in different parts of the world.

We know much more about locoweed poisoning, although the problem is vastly more complex. The word *loco* is Spanish for "crazy" and was applied because of the symptoms exhibited by poisoned horses. Loco occurs in horses, cattle, sheep, and goats on ranges of the Rocky Mountain states westward to the Pacific. It has caused severe loss of life in range livestock, and was investigated by the Department of Agriculture as early as 1873. Horses were the major means of human transportation in the Old West and a locoed horse put the life of its rider in danger.

The disease is complex and was confused with others for many years. A month or more of poisoning is required before symptoms appear. During that time animals, especially horses, may travel widely. This makes relating symptoms to ingestion of a particular kind of plant especially difficult. Moreover, it has been learned that several species of two different plants (*Astragalus* and *Oxytropis*) are involved in loco poisoning and that *other* species of *Astragalus* (which has perhaps 300 species) are toxic in other ways. Some species of *Astragalus* are harmless and furnish desirable forage on ranges, yet it is practically impossible for anyone but a botanical specialist to tell many of the species apart.

Despite these difficulties, we know the incidence of loco and the economic loss caused by it each year; the species of animals which are poisoned; the conditions which predispose to poisoning and ways of controlling it; the identity of most, if not all, the species of *Astragalus* and *Oxytropis* which can produce loco and their general relative toxicity; the amount of plant necessary to produce symptoms and death; the time required for the disease to develop; and the detailed nature of symptoms and how they vary in different animals from onset to death or recovery. Something of how the poisonous principle works is understood. The gross lesions are known in detail, and certain changes have been found in cells of the brain, which may be responsible for the nervous symptoms. We know that final paralysis is caused by damage in the brain. And finally a lot is known about the chemical nature of the poisonous principle, although some question remains as to its exact structure.

The proper investigation of a poisonous plant is a complex procedure, involving many professional talents. We now recognize the need for accurate identification of the plant involved (by a taxonomic botanist) and of the toxic compound (by an analytical, organic chemist). Also required are accurate and detailed descriptions of symptoms and gross lesions (by a physician, veterinarian, veterinary or medical clinician, or pathologist) and (by histologist or pathologist) of the microscopic changes the poisonous compound has produced in animal tissues. Professional experiments with laboratory animals must be repeatedly carried out during chemical analysis to determine which fractions are toxic. Only after all of these aspects have been studied can recommendations be made which will prevent further loss of life. In the case of livestock, the professional knowledge of the agronomist, animal husbandman, range ecologist, or the like may be required. Obviously it is not easy to conduct a thorough investigation of a poisonous plant, nor is it inexpensive; consequently it is infrequently accomplished.

Investigations reported in respected scientific and professional journals are the only reliable sources to use in protecting human and animal life. Experience shows that information found in occasional newspaper reports of cases of poisoning cannot be used as the basis for describing the toxicity of a plant. However, they often point to places where experimental investigations are needed.

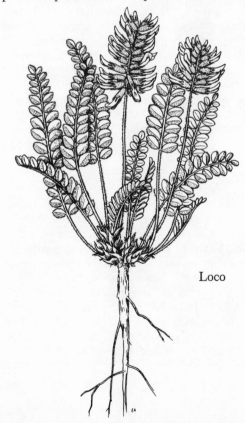

Loco

3
Where
Is
Toxicity?

It would be convenient, indeed, if toxicity were confined to a certain group or even to several groups within the plant kingdom. Discovering them, we could safely neglect the rest. Some plant families such as the legumes (Leguminosae) and rose family (Rosaceae), commonly thought to be particularly dangerous, do contain many species which are poisonous; but each also contains many species not poisonous at all, while other poisonous species are found scattered in many other families. How much pattern is there in botanical distribution of poisonous substances? How is toxicity distributed among the various parts of a plant as it germinates, grows, and matures? How specific is the reaction of different kinds of animals to a given poison? Do some geographic areas have many poisonous plants while others are relatively free of them? What is the environmental distribution of toxicity? Are pastures more toxic than home gardens, for instance?

Where is toxicity within the plant kingdom?

Practically all major classes of plants contain poisonous members. Toxicity is entirely lacking so far only in some groups of algae, some fungi, and the mosses. These groups are either composed of small individual plants not likely to be consumed in quantity because of their size, or they live in habitats which make them more or less unavailable as articles of diet for either man or animals.

Although poison-forming bacteria are less important than those that are infectious, one, *Clostridium botulinum*, excretes a toxin, chemically much like the phytotoxin of the precatory bean. Ingestion of this toxin produces botulism or food poisoning. *Clostridium botulinum* is sometimes found in spoiled home-canned produce where its toxin accumulates in the food. It is particularly dangerous not only because of the potency of the poison it excretes, but also because the food spoilage it causes is not accompanied by production of gas, strong odor, or unusual taste and is, therefore, not readily detected. Fortunately, thorough boiling inactivates the toxin.

There are several different kinds of poisonous fungi. Deadly mushrooms or toadstools come first to mind, but smuts, rusts, and other fungi of decay can cause poisoning in various ways. The ergot fungus has already been described. Compared with the total number of species of mushrooms, the poisonous ones are few. Nevertheless, the deadliness of some of the toxic mushrooms has been recognized from very early times, and separating poisonous ones from edible ones is not easy. Popular "rules" for distinguishing poisonous mushrooms from edible ones are dangerous. The persistence of these "rules" despite repeated authoritative public warnings against them is hard to explain. Other than absolute, correct identification of the mushroom in question no single rule, characteristic, or procedure exists which allows a poisonous species to be distinguished from one that is not. Many deaths may be laid to use of these "rules."

One such "rule" states that if the skin can be peeled from the cap of a mushroom, it is nonpoisonous. The skin may easily be peeled from the cap of *Amanita muscaria*, fly agaric, one of the commonest poisonous mushrooms in the United States. Even more frequently encountered is the statement that a silver spoon or coin added to the pan in which mushrooms are cooked will darken if poisonous species are present. This is not so. Deadly amanita, or destroying angel (*Amanita phalloides*), the most dangerous species of mushroom in this country, will not cause silver to darken, nor, probably, will any *fresh* mushroom.

Occasionally, dangerous confusion arises from differences in the way people use the terms "mushroom" and "toadstool." For some people "toadstool" means that the fungus is poisonous, while for others "mushroom" and "toadstool" are entirely synonomous and neither carries any particular implication of toxicity. Don't rely on these terms, therefore, to separate poisonous from non-poisonous species.

Mushrooms are difficult to identify. Even the specialists disagree on the identification of species in the genus *Amanita*. Amanitas probably account for 90 per cent or more of the cases of lethal poisoning by mushrooms in the United States, yet a few species of this genus are among those most prized by connoisseurs of edible fungi. Most mushrooms have stem and cap with gills radially organized and pendant within or beneath the cap. In some, instead of gills, the flesh of the cap is penetrated by thousands of pores opening to the underside. Both groups contain poisonous members. A small number of rarer, stalked fungi bear, in place of the cap, a fleshy mass whose surface is composed of a coarse open network of ridges and valleys. The prized edible morel is among the latter, but at least one, the false morel, is poisonous under some conditions of growth. The point is, no one can assume that a fungus of the pore-bearing type or of the morel type is nonpoisonous simply because it belongs to those groups.

Not all mushrooms have yet been tested for toxicity. One mushroom (*Galerina venenata*), for example, had never even been previously found, described, or named until 1953, when a case of near-lethal poisoning brought it to the attention of botanists specializing in fungi.

Variation in toxicity among mushrooms seems greater than among other species of poisonous plants. Some mushrooms are reported to be highly toxic to some persons in some places while entirely nontoxic under other circumstances. For all these reasons, the rule I recommend, and follow in my own household, is that no wild mushroom shall be eaten unless it has been identified beyond a shadow of doubt as one of the species known to be wholesome, and then, only if it is absolutely fresh. Necessity for freshness should, of course, apply to all foods one eats, but is especially important for fungi. These plants produce a large number and variety of compounds from which toxic molecules may form spontaneously with time or through decay.

Everyone should know the characteristics of an *Amanita*, which accounts for most cases of lethal mushroom poisoning of man. Amanitas are typical mushrooms with stem, cap, and gills. They are relatively large, but the exact size varies with the species and with the specimen. The cap is globular or conical in the very young mushroom but opens out, and becomes flat or even slightly upturned at the rim in fully expanded specimens. Gills are white in *fresh* Amanitas. (They are clearly brown in the common edible, cultivated or field mushroom.) The base of the stem is distinctly bulbous and is often well buried in the ground. Great care must be taken to dig it out before judging this characteristic because the stem is easily broken. The upper portion of the base (where it nar-

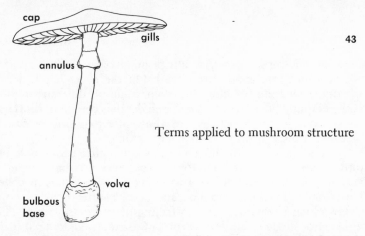

Terms applied to mushroom structure

rows to the diameter of the rest of the stem) is prolonged upward as free edge or a thin membranous lip encircling the stem, or as an irregularly broken circle of upwardly directed scalelike elements. This structure is called by some the "death's cup" (technically, the "volva"), but it is found on some mushrooms which are not poisonous. Higher up on the stem, in the shadow of the cap, a very delicate, hanging, veil-like membrane, the "annulus," encircles the stem. This is part of the remains of a thin veil of tissue which surrounds the unopened cap in young specimens. It is sometimes not found in older specimens, having been lost because of its delicate nature. The veil over the cap surface does not stretch as the cap expands, but instead is ruptured irregularly into small flecks of tissue which usually remain stuck to the upper surface of the expanded cap as small thin patches. Like the annulus, these are sometimes lost in mature specimens and tend to be absent or nearly so in some species. Otherwise the surface of the cap is usually smooth and dry. Three characteristics should be especially well remembered: bulbous base, annulus, and white gills. Each of these may be found in an edible species and all three together in some; nevertheless, the novice should reject mushrooms with these characteristics.

Amanitas usually grow in groups, but sometimes singly, in open woods, or brushy areas of pastures. They vary in color from yellow to orange, brown, reddish, olive, and chalky white. Amanitas are common throughout the United States, although different species may be found in different areas.

The nature of poisoning by *Amanita* depends on the species. Some are entirely harmless. Other species (for example, *Amanita muscaria*, the fly mushroom or fly agaric) produce symptoms of severe digestive upset, which usually begin less than three hours after ingestion, but results are rarely fatal. On the other hand, deadly amanita (*Amanita phalloides*), containing a different poison, produces quite different symptoms, and death is common. Mortality ranges from 50 to 90 per cent of those affected. One or two of these mushrooms can kill even after cooking.

A case is known in which a child was killed after eating only one third of one cap. This high toxicity presents unusual danger of poisoning from a specimen or two mixed in with others in collections from the wild. Symptoms appear only after 6 to 15 hours during which the patient has no feeling of anything wrong. They begin as a sudden, intense seizure of extreme abdominal pain, with vomiting and diarrhea. The poison damages the liver and, in later stages, jaundice may appear. Paroxysms of pain and vomiting alternate with period of remission over 6 to 8 days (less in children) before death or slow recovery. Periods of remission become longer toward the end, but the case may still result in death (especially if treatment is relaxed because the lengthening remissions are interpreted as indicating that the patient is out of danger).

Many other species of mushrooms, of many types, descriptions, and habitats, are mildly or severely poisonous. The diseases they cause vary greatly. Even well-experienced collectors of wild mushrooms have sometimes been poisoned. We repeat that the only safe rule is to eat only those mushrooms which have been identified beyond doubt, and which are known to be wholesome.

Fly agaric (*Amanita muscaria*)

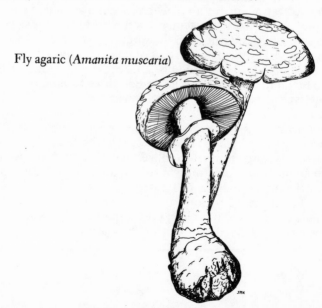

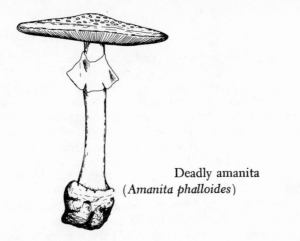

Deadly amanita
(*Amanita phalloides*)

Poisonings caused by rusts and smuts are found in animals which have been fed spoiled grains or which have obtained the fungi from molded bedding. In most cases the toxic compound is produced entirely by the fungus; in others it is the product of joint action between the host plant and fungus and will not be formed by either alone.

Algae are primitive photosynthetic plants, often microscopic in size, which inhabit natural waters. Common terms such as pond scum, frog spit, plankton, seaweed (and sometimes "moss") usually refer to algal types of plant life. Like the fungi, the algae are composed of a number of more or less distantly related groups of organisms. Of these, chiefly two, the blue-green algae and the dinoflagellates, have toxic members.

Toxic blue-green algae grow in ponds and lakes, particularly those rich in nutrients. Poisoning occurs only if these microscopic plants collect in vast concentrations as they sometimes do after a period of hot, sunny weather which promotes their growth and constant prevailing winds from one direction which cause them to collect on the lee side of the lake. Rarely will lake waters become toxic until populations of algae reach such numbers that they are clearly evident in the water. Dangerous waters usually look like thin blue or gray paint. Toxic species of algae form small, almost microscopic colonies which may be just visible as tiny flecks of dull green in a handful of pond water. Types of algae which form mats composed of intertangled threads floating on the surface of ponds are not toxic.

Nearly a dozen species of blue-green algae have been identified in cases of animal toxicity. Most of them fall in three common genera, *Anabaena, Aphanizomenon,* and *Microcystis* (known as Annie, Fannie, and Mike among some waterworks officials). The few cases of poisoning of human beings which might have been caused by blue-green algae are not conclusive. On the other hand, cattle, sheep, horses, swine, dogs, cats, fowl, geese, wild and domestic ducks, game and songbirds, fish, rodents, and small game have been killed, sometimes in large numbers, by drinking water containing toxic blue-green algae. This is one of the rare sources of serious poisoning in wild animals. Poisoning of man from blue-green algae is unlikely for two reasons. First, public-health and municipal-water-supply authorities are well aware of, and constantly testing for, these dangerous organisms in public water supplies; and secondly, it is unlikely that anyone would drink from or swim in water discolored with dangerous concentrations of blue-green algae.

Dinoflagellates are microscopic, brownish, single-celled organisms which sometimes form extensive populations in marine or fresh waters. They are dangerous to man only because they are one of the principal food supplies of clams, oysters, some crabs, and other marine organisms employed as food by man. Only a few species (especially *Gonyaulax catenella* and *Gonyaulax tamarensis*) are toxic and these contain a nerve toxin somewhat like curare in its effect.

The toxin accumulates in the tissues of marine mollusks. These shellfish feed by filtering dinoflagellates and other microscopic organisms from the water. Surprisingly the poison is not toxic to mollusks, even in very high concentration. The mollusks, however, become highly toxic to man and other warm-blooded animals.

As few as six toxic clams have killed an adult man. Poisoning has occurred on the West Coast from California to Alaska and on the East Coast in the Bay of Fundy and St. Lawrence River mouth areas. Hundreds of cases of severe poisoning and death in man have been recorded since the first on the West Coast in 1798. Governments of the United States and Canada have, for some years, maintained extensive sampling and testing programs which have been fully effective in spotting populations of toxic shellfish. Warning notices are placed in newspapers and dangerous areas are posted to prevent "digging." Where such warnings are ignored, patrols may be maintained. Some persons are capable of ignoring all such warnings and cases of death still occur occasionally. Areas closed to shellfishing because of toxicity, pollution, or to protect against

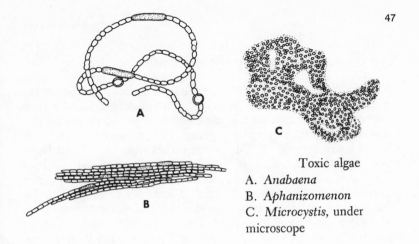

Toxic algae
A. *Anabaena*
B. *Aphanizomenon*
C. *Microcystis,* under
microscope

destruction of shellfish populations should be scrupulously avoided.

Symptoms of shellfish poisoning in man appear in a few hours and consist of numbness or a "pins and needles" feeling about the face and in the finger tips, nausea, loss of control over the body and speech, headache, and finally general paralysis and collapse. If the patient survives the first twenty-four hours, he may be expected to recover. Shellfish are made less toxic by cooking.

"Red tides" along the Florida coast and elsewhere are the result of accumulations of populations of another dinoflagellate, *Gymnodinium brevis* ("Jim brevis" to some), the individual cells of which become so numerous that color is imparted to the water. This organism contains a poison which has caused mass mortality of fish, and almost the total fish population has been killed in some areas. Furthermore, tiny droplets of water containing a toxic substance from the dinoflagellate occasionally get into the air and cause coughing and choking in human populations within a few miles of the shore. This effect is apparently harmless and usually disappears rapidly when the wind changes. Investigators are now trying to determine the conditions which bring about blooms of dinoflagellates so that they may be controlled in the future.

These examples illustrate types of toxicity to be found among various groups of bacteria, fungi, and algae. An idea of the even more complex distribution of toxicity in the remainder of the plant kingdom can be gained from the list of plants, arranged according to their natural relationships, in the appendix.

Toxicity and closeness of plant relationship

Though there is little definite evidence one way or the other, as a generalization, it seems true that plants closely enough related to be considered species of the same genus possess similar toxicity.

There are exceptions to this generalization, however, and the exceptions are important. The genus *Eupatorium* contains a large number of species, many of which are common weeds. White snakeroot is one of the white-flowered species, but some 30 other eupatoriums are also white-flowered. These species are so closely alike that the botanist must use small differences in flower structure, visible with hand lens, to separate them. Nevertheless, white snakeroot is singled out from all the other eupatoriums by its toxicity.

White snakeroot has had more than minor importance in American history. The greatly feared disease of human beings called milk sickness, characterized by weakness, nausea, and prostration, has been known since the time of the American Revolution. It occasionally reached epidemic proportions in certain areas of the United States, locally and sporadically causing loss of human life second to no other disease. In time it was associated with using milk from cattle suffering from a disease termed "trembles." These associated diseases of livestock and human beings were first reported from North Carolina and seemed to follow the settlers westward into the central states as they were inhabited. Milk sickness reached a peak in incidence during the first half of the nineteenth century. It was so devastating in some areas that the human population was

White snakeroot

reduced to less than one half its original number in a single year or two. On some occasions entire villages were abandoned, for it had been learned through painful experience that milk sickness occurred only in certain limited areas. This disease was reputedly responsible for the death of Nancy Hanks, Abraham Lincoln's mother.

Great in number and ingenuity were the explanations offered for milk sickness. Poisonous plants were incriminated from the first, and more than a score of individual plants received blame at one time or another. Poison ivy was one of the chief contenders. On the other hand, some people believed that milk sickness and trembles were caused by miasmas arising from the soil, from spider webs, or from other equally improbable sources, viewed from the vantage of the twentieth century. When bacteria were discovered to produce disease, milk sickness was blamed on them, but it proved impossible in controlled tests to isolate any which could cause it. Before the true explanation could be determined, milk sicknesss first had to be clearly associated with use of milk from animals with trembles, and second, trembles had to be clearly associated with ingestion of snakeroot.

The first was complicated by the fact that the poisonous compound is concentrated in the milk of lactating animals (snakeroot poisoning is almost unique in this respect), so that persons using the poisoned milk often show symptoms before the cow does. The second was made difficult by the fact that trembles develops very slowly. Fairly large amounts of snakeroot must be eaten by cattle over several days or longer before poisoning appears.

Another difficulty rose in recognizing white snakeroot from closely related or similar-appearing plants. Snakeroot grows throughout much of North America in moist soils of open woods, or about the edges of woods. When the lands were initially cleared, white snakeroot often made extensive stands in the first few years before the soil was thoroughly worked. When in flower, it is a showy herbaceous perennial weed, with stiff, unbranched or branching stems, mostly 3 to 4 feet tall. The leaves are opposite on the stem, with oval or heart-shaped blades borne on long stalks. The tissue of the blades is thin and the edge is coarsely cut into points. Three main veins are particularly evident on the under surface. The flowers are tiny, white, and grouped in great number, so that the flowering mass, produced at the tips of the branches, has a lacy, airy, delicate effect.

The toxic principle is unique. After much work it was isolated by chemists of the United States Department of Agriculture, and found to be a hydrocarbon compound with the chemical characteristics of an alcohol. They named it tremetol from the name of the disease it caused in animals. The toxic molecule is especially soluble in fats, accounting for its concentration in milk, and, as found later, in butter. It causes a fundamental upset in the biochemistry of metabolism (the burning of food and use of resulting energy) in the cells of the body. Among other things, abnormal amounts of acetonelike compounds are formed. Acetone is a volatile compound with a characteristic, readily apparent odor that is partially excreted in the breath. Physicians of older days, it is said, could diagnose a case of milk sickness upon entering the house by the distinctive, pervading odor.

At the present time cases of milk sickness in human beings are rare, although an occasional case of trembles in cattle may still be found. Conscientious dairymen reject milk from sick animals. Even if they didn't, it would normally be pooled with milk from other animals in the same herd and from herds over a wide geographic area during handling, pasteurizing, and bottling. The toxic factor would thus be diluted far below the levels at which harm might result. The only danger to man is from the family cow. White snakeroot is still common, but under the agricultural practices now followed, it is unusual to find more than a few plants in places where cattle have access to them.

White snakeroot is an example of a poisonous plant which has many closely related nonpoisonous species. Of all the species of *Eupatorium*, only one other has toxicity. *Eupatorium wrightii* (no common name) has been incriminated in unexplained loss of cattle, but from the characteristics of the disease, the toxic compound is not the tremetol found in white snakeroot.

Even when, as usual, species of a genus have roughly similar toxicity, it is often important to know exactly which species is involved in a case of poisoning. The common Eastern milkweed possesses only slight toxicity, at most, yet some of the Western species of milkweed are among the most toxic plants known, and even among them some species may be one hundred or more times as toxic as others. Labriform milkweed, for instance, is extremely toxic. Ingestion of five hundredths of a pound of plant per 100 pounds of animal weight brings on symptoms. Several other Western milkweeds are moderately toxic; about 1 pound of plant

Labriform milkweed

per 100 pounds of animal weight produces symptoms. Knowing the species thus makes it possible to estimate the danger, which in turn may determine the measures to be taken to avoid further poisoning. So far as we know, none of these plants has been responsible for poisoning man (it is unlikely that anyone would consume them), but they have caused extensive losses among livestock.

Different genera, even in the same family, are usually unrelated in toxicity. The majority of genera in families such as the grasses and legumes are harmless and many are important as sources of food. Each of these families, however, contains some toxic plants.

In some plant families the toxic genera *all* contain the same general toxic principle. In the rose family, for example, all the toxic members, such as mountain mahogany, apple, wild cherries, peaches, and almonds, contain cyanogenetic glycosides.

Another example is the heath family, the toxic members of which include mountain laurels, Labrador tea, Sierra laurel, rusty-leaf, pieris, and rhododendron. The poisonous compound in all of these is andromedotoxin, a resinoid carbohydrate.

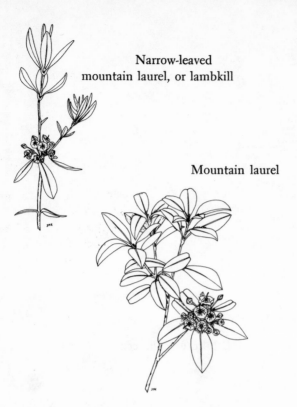

Narrow-leaved
mountain laurel, or lambkill

Mountain laurel

The Delaware Indians used laurel for suicide. "Tea" made from as little as 2 ounces of leaves has produced poisoning in man. Livestock and wild animals have repeatedly been poisoned by these plants. Zoo animals are particularly liable to poisoning because laurels and rhododendrons are frequently used as ornamental plants in the grounds of zoos, and persons unaware of their toxicity are apt to feed the leaves to them. Cemetery wreaths and stage decorations made from laurels have been lethal to other animals.

Symptoms of laurel poisoning usually appear in about 6 hours. Excess salivation, nausea, and vomiting are usually found, together with severe abdominal pain.

The heath family is a large one with several hundred species. All of the poisonous species fall into two of its subfamilies. Laurels and rhododendrons, widely used in landscaping, are readily recognized by most persons. Their persistent, leathery leaves are particularly characteristic. The other poisonous heaths, especially those which drop their leaves in winter, are not as easily recognized, but in season the showy flowers help in their identification.

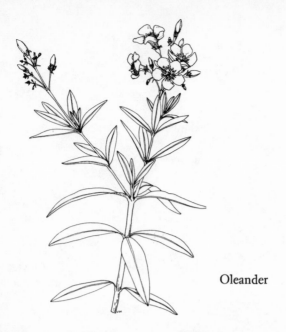

Oleander

In the closely related milkweed and dogbane families, the nature of the poisonous compounds remains largely undetermined, though several have been shown to be present in each family.

Two bad actors in the dogbane family are oleander and the several dogbanes. Oleander grows into a large shrub. It is commonly cultivated outdoors in the South and in California, and occasionally is used indoors. Often, in Victorian times, an oleander plant was kept at the foot of the stairway in the front hall whence its heavy perfume pervaded the house. At one time it was believed that the cloyingly sweet odor from a flowering oleander was dangerous and might poison a person in a closed, unventilated room. This is not the case, but the persistent, leathery leaves and wood of oleander are, indeed, dangerous. Sometimes a branch from an oleander bush is cut to skewer meat at an outdoor picnic. The poison of the plant is transferred into the meat, often with fatal result.

What we thought we knew about the toxicity of the dogbanes, which was considerable, turns out to be largely the result of an error. Confusion of common names in a bulletin from one of the Southwestern state experiment stations mixed up results obtained from oleander experiments with the dogbanes which have been little experimented with. Consequently the dogbanes, though undoubtedly poisonous, have been masquerading under false statistics for nearly half a century.

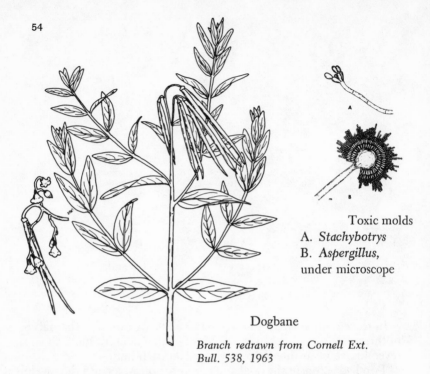

Toxic molds
A. *Stachybotrys*
B. *Aspergillus,*
under microscope

Dogbane

Branch redrawn from Cornell Ext.
Bull. 538, 1963

Toxicity is sometimes expressed even at the level of the individual isolate. Poisoning of livestock by molded corn has been a problem in some areas. Research to discover the identity of the fungus involved showed that the molds *Stachybotrys atra* and *Aspergillus flavus* were responsible, but in each case, only certain individual isolates had capacity to produce toxicity. Other isolates of the same species were nontoxic even though grown under identical conditions.

Often a plant species is separable into several varieties, which rarely differ in toxicity. An exception is jimmy fern of the Southwest. One variety of this fern (*cochisensis*) produces a nervous disease, called jimmies, in sheep. Another variety (*sinuata*) of the same species, tested carefully under equivalent circumstances, does not produce toxicity at all.

Plant breeders have developed many strains of cultivated plants in which certain desirable characteristics have been emphasized by breeding and selection. Among them are strains of sudan grass in which the capacity to form cyanide has been significantly reduced. Use of these strains has nearly eliminated the possibility of live-

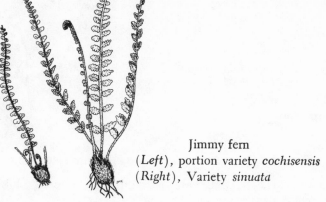

Jimmy fern
(*Left*), portion variety *cochisensis*
(*Right*), Variety *sinuata*

stock poisoning which occurred occasionally when animals were pastured on immature or drought-stunted sudan grass.

Natural hybrids sometimes occur when a plant of one species crosses with a closely related species. Usually the characteristics of the hybrid are intermediate between those of the parents. In 1936 a plant, apparently a hybrid, was discovered in Argentina. It has some of the characteristics of sudan grass and some of Johnson grass, and has been named *Sorghum almum*. Johnson grass is a common, aggressive, perennial weed of Southern states, capable of producing cyanide poisoning in livestock which graze on it. It has been declared a noxious weed by law in many states and it must not be present in agricultural seed offered for sale.

The Argentine plant has some of the desirable characteristics of sudan grass and ease of culture of Johnson grass, but it also has a high cyanide potential. Furthermore, the seed of *Sorghum almum* cannot be distinguished from that of Johnson grass. For this reason many agricultural specialists have resisted the introduction of *Sorghum almum* (under commercial names such as Columbus grass) for agricultural use in the Southern states. Other artificially produced hybrids between Johnson grass and sudan grass which have been selected for low cyanide potential and other desirable characteristics offer greater promise. These selections have been given names such as perennial sweet sudan grass and sorgrass.

Individual plants may differ in the accumulation of selenium. Some species avidly accumulate this element from soils where it is found, concentrating it in their tissues a thousandfold or more. Plants which have such a capacity become highly toxic to animals which graze them. Furthermore, they may change the form of the

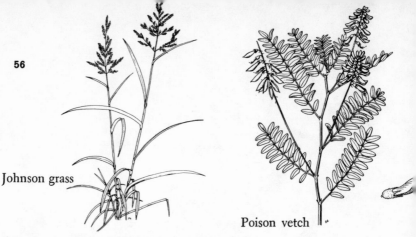

Johnson grass

Poison vetch

selenium as they take it from the soil, making it more soluble and hence more dangerous.

Accumulating plants are of two general types. Some, for reasons as yet unknown, will not grow where selenium is absent in the soil. They seem to require this element, although no good reason is known why they should. They are sometimes called selenium indicator plants. Because selenium and uranium tend to be found in similar geological formations, selenium indicator plants have become important to the uranium prospector. Contrast the prospector of old—his grubstake, burro, pickax and practiced eye—with the modern uranium prospector, equipped with Jeep or airplane, Geiger counter, and practiced eye, the latter peeled for certain plants!

The other type of selenium-accumulating plant can take it or leave it. Such plants take up selenium from soils where the element is present, but grow just as well where there is no trace of it.

Selenium occurs in several forms in soils and rocks of geological formations from Pennsylvanian (about 300 million years ago) to the present. Such soils are found in 15 of the Western states, Hawaii, and western Canada. Soils rarely contain more than 100 parts selenium per million parts soil, but some rocks have been found to contain about 1,500 ppm. selenium. Accumulating plants may contain concentrations up to 15,000 parts selenium per million parts of plant. About a score of the approximately 300 species of *Astragalus* mentioned earlier are known to accumulate selenium. They are commonly called "poison vetch."

All accumulating plants are members of the native range vegetation in the areas where they grow. Usually they are avoided by livestock, but if not, they may produce one of three different types of poisoning, depending (in a way not yet fully understood) on the amount and chemical form of selenium that is ingested. These include acute selenium poisoning which is rare; "alkali disease," in which emaciation, hoof deformity, and lameness are major symptoms; and "blind staggers," which involves blindness, excitement, and other nervous symptoms.

Plants which accumulate large concentrations of selenium are rarely dangerous to man because he doesn't eat them. Some food plants, however, may passively take up enough selenium from high-selenium soils to become potentially dangerous. Many agricultural plants, especially grain crops, are in this category. Though crops grown on Western soils usually are perfectly harmless, soils of a few small areas contain soluble selenium in sufficient concentration so that grains grown on them may provoke in man a disease similar to "alkali disease" in livestock. These soils have been subject to detailed investigation by the Department of Agriculture, their boundaries are well established, and constant check is maintained so that grains grown on them are not used in any way that might be harmful to man.

One other characteristic of selenium poisoning brings us back to the possible toxicity of an individual plant when other individuals in the same species are nontoxic. Such a situation may arise, for example, when a selenium-accumulating species dies, drops its leaves, or is plowed into the soil. The selenium concentrated in it is returned to the soil directly about the plant, increasing the concentration of soluble selenium many times in that particular spot. Any plant subsequently growing in that spot may, if it is not killed by selenium, passively absorb enough of it to become toxic even though other plants of the same species, perhaps growing within a few feet of the toxic specimen, remain nontoxic.

Sleepy grass

Some species of plants are poisonous only when growing within limited geographical areas. The toxicity of sleepy grass, for example, does not seem to depend on the presence of a chemical element in the soil. Sleepy grass, a coarse perennial which grows from Colorado to Texas, Arizona, and Mexico, is poisonous, according to Department of Agriculture experiments, only in limited geographic areas of the Sacramento and Sierra Blanca Mountains of New Mexico.

Expeditions depending on horses for transportation in the early days often had great difficulty traveling through these areas of New Mexico because their horses ate the grass readily and moderate amounts of it produce profound, nearly stuporous sleep. The condition lasts several days, during which it is impossible to rouse the animals more than momentarily. A poisonous principle capable of producing such deep sleep of animals might have great medical value, but attempts by pharmaceutical companies to extract an effective compound have been unsuccessful.

In general, no major part of the plant kingdom is free from toxic plants. The close relationship of one plant with another of known toxicity makes us suspicious, but does not necessarily prove the first also is toxic.

Toxicity as related to part of plant or stage of growth

Are all parts of a plant equally toxic? Are plants equally toxic throughout their growing seasons? The answer depends on the particular plant. Often—probably in the majority of instances—not enough information is at hand to prove whether all parts of a plant are equally toxic or whether the plant maintains the same toxicity throughout its growing period. We assume that they are unless there is evidence to the contrary.

Let's consider water hemlock, one of the most poisonous of all plants. This plant is known by many common names in different parts of the country. It is called cowbane, wild parsnip, snakeroot, snakeweed, beaver poison, muskrat weed, spotted hemlock, spotted cowbane, musquash root, false parsley, poison hemlock, wild carrot, fever root, mock-eel root, spotted parsley, and *carotte à moreau* in French Canada. The profusion of common names, the confusion with other poisonous plants, indicates the difficulty in recognizing this plant. This is particularly unfortunate because water hemlock is considered by many authorities the most virulent poisonous plant of the North Temperate Zone.

Water hemlock.
Young plant in early spring;
lengthwise cut through stem
base; mature leaflet veins

The genus *Cicuta* to which water hemlock belongs has several closely related species distributed in various parts of the country. All appear about equally toxic. They are members of the carrot family and are difficult to distinguish from some of the other members of the same family.

The important characteristics to look for include the following: Water hemlock grows in moist habitats such as in marshes or along stream banks. The habitat may not remain moist throughout the year, but must be moist or inundated at some time to support good growth of plants. The first foliage that appears in the spring is a cluster of leaves arising from a single point at the surface of the ground. Each leaf attains a length of one to three feet and is composed of many leaflets which, to the inexperienced person, look like separate small leaves. The leaflets are relatively long and narrow, tapering to a sharp tip. Each is 2 to 5 inches long and the edge of the blade is composed of many sharp pointed teeth.

A central main vein runs the length of the leaflet. Secondary veins arise from opposite sides of the main vein and run toward the edges of the leaflet. In most plants, secondary veins with this arrangement end in the points at the edge of the leaflet. In water hemlock *the secondary veins end in the valleys or notches between points.* In some cases they split just before reaching the notch and do not actually touch it, but in all cases their course is clearly toward the notch as opposed to the tip of the tooth.

The main stem of the plant is produced only during flowering which occurs in late spring or early summer. The flowers are tiny, white or greenish, and are grouped into a mass which resembles the inflorescence of Queen Anne's lace or wild carrot with which most persons are familiar. The flowering stem may be 5 to 10 feet tall and bears smaller leaves than those forming the clump at ground level.

The most characteristic part of the water hemlock plant is its root system. The main roots are thickened and occur in a bunch attached at a single point to the thickened base of the stem. They look much like a clump of dahlia roots, but are smaller. Each is approximately 1 to 3 inches long and about a half inch or a little more in diameter. Usually two to five are found on each plant, but weak specimens may have only one. It is difficult to tell exactly where the roots are attached to the stem since the basal inch or more of stem is thickened and resembles the roots.

If the basal, thickened portion of the stem is cut in half lengthwise, a characteristic structure will be seen: The cut surface displays a number of horizontal yellow lines across the delicate pith. In older specimens, if the basal portion of the stem has begun to elongate, the pith is torn apart and the yellow lines, somewhat farther apart now, are separated by air chambers. Each is formed by a thin diaphragm of tissue stretched across the diameter of the thickened stem. Shortly after the cut surface is exposed to the air, tiny yellowish drops of sap usually form on it. The odor is distinctive, not unlike that of freshly cut carrot or parsnip, but sufficiently different so that a person who has experienced it can tell water hemlock from the others by odor.

The thickened roots serve as food-storage reservoirs for the plant. The food in each cluster of roots is exhausted as the flowering stem is produced, but the foliage lasts and manufactures more food through the remainder of the season. A new cluster of roots is formed as an offset from the original in this process and remains in the ground over the winter when the original plant dies. In the spring it gives rise to a new clump of foliage and soon to a new flowering stem. Each individual plant, then, lives usually only one year, but because of the method of root propagation, a population of plants tends to remain in the same place from year to year. New populations are also formed by seeds which germinate readily and are effective in distributing the plant.

The roots are the chief toxic portion of the plant. As little as one mouthful may kill a man. The plant gets its reputation as our most virulent poisonous plant, however, more from the violence of the symptoms it produces than from its degree of toxicity, which is matched or exceeded by that of several other poisonous plants. The toxic principle is a higher, largely unsaturated alcohol nearly unique to water hemlock; it is found also in *Oenanthe,* a British plant. It is a violent convulsant. There is a vivid description, written in Latin in 1679, of a case of water hemlock poisoning that occurred in Europe and England in the 1600's:[3]

When about the end of March, 1670 the cattle were being led from the village to water at the spring, in treading the river banks they exposed the roots of this *Cicuta* [water hemlock], whose stems and leaf buds were now coming forth. At that time two boys and six girls, a little before noon, ran out to the spring and the meadow through which the river flows, and seeing a root and thinking that it was a golden parsnip, not through the bidding of any evil appetite, but at the behest of wayward frolicsomeness, ate greedily of it, and certain of the girls among them commended the root to the others for its sweetness and pleasantness, wherefore the boys, especially, ate quite abundantly of it and joyfully hastened home; and one of the girls tearfully complained to her mother that she had been supplied too meagerly by her comrades, with the root.

Jacob Maeder, a boy of six years, possessed of white locks, and delicate though active, returned home happy and smiling, as if things had gone well. A little while afterwards he complained of pain in his abdomen, and, scarcely uttering a word, fell prostrate on the ground, and urinated with great violence to the heighth of a man. Presently he was a terrible sight to see, being seized with convulsions, with the loss of all his senses. His mouth was shut most tightly so that it could not be opened by any means. He grated his teeth; he twisted his eyes about strangely and blood flowed from his ears. In the region of his abdomen a certain swollen body of the size of a man's fist struck the hand of the afflicted father with the greatest force, particularly in the neighborhood of the ensiform cartilage. He frequently hiccupped; at times he seemed to be about to vomit, but he could force nothing from his mouth, which was most tightly closed. He tossed his limbs about marvelously and twisted them; frequently his head was drawn backward and his whole back was curved in the form of a bow, so that a small child could have crept beneath him in the space between his back and the bed without touching him. When the convulsions ceased momentarily, he implored the assistance of his mother. Presently, when they returned with equal violence, he could be aroused by no pinching, by no talking, or by no other means, until his strength failed and he grew pale; and when a hand was placed on his breast he breathed his

[3] C. A. Jacobson, "Water Hemlock (*Cicuta*)." Nevada Agricultural Experiment Station, Technical Bulletin 81, 1915.

last. These symptoms continued scarcely beyond a half hour. After
his death, his abdomen and face swelled without lividness except that
a little was noticeable about the eyes. From the mouth of the corpse
even to the hour of his burial green froth flowed very abundantly, and
although it was wiped away frequently by his grieving father, nevertheless new froth soon took its place.

Scores of persons, especially children, have been killed by this
plant in the United States. The fleshy roots are attractive to children
and have been mistaken by adults for edible roots such as those of
wild parsnip or wild artichoke. The roots are poisonous at all stages
of growth except the very youngest and even the old, dead, exhausted
roots may retain some toxicity. The very young growth coming from
the roots in the spring also is toxic, but the older growth apparently
loses toxicity rapidly. There is little danger in the foliage of a mature
plant.

Most loss of life, both of livestock and of man, occurs in early
spring because at that time the roots are most easily removed from
the moist soil. Plants are frequently washed out of stream banks and
roots are strewn downstream. Poisoning by this plant is among the
most difficult to diagnose, since so little plant is required. The offending roots may have been picked up at a distance from the place
where they originally grew or the entire evidence may have been
consumed by the poisoned subject. It is wise to commit to memory
the three major characteristics which help one to recognize water
hemlock: secondary veins proceeding to notches rather than to
points of leaflets; chambered rootstock with horizontal diaphragms
of yellow tissue in the pith; and clustered fleshy roots, sometimes
only one, growing from the rootstock.

A word should be said here about several other plants which are
called hemlock. Poison hemlock contains a toxic compound entirely
different from that in water hemlock. The native yew, often called
ground hemlock, also is poisonous, yet its symptoms are unlike those
produced by either water hemlock or poison hemlock. The hemlock
tree is not known to be poisonous at all.

Poison hemlock is a European plant which was introduced into
this hemisphere many years ago and now is well established as a
weed throughout the United States and Canada. It grows in the
same kind of habitat as Queen Anne's lace or wild carrot, which it
resembles in leaves and inflorescence. It is a coarse plant, nearly
3 feet tall before flowering. The flowering stem may be 6 feet or more

in height. Like water hemlock and wild carrot, it is a member of the carrot family.

Poison hemlock has lacy foliage, most of which arises in a clump at ground level. When the flowering stem is produced later in the season, it bears additional leaves and rounded carrotlike inflorescences, at the top. Each leaf is divided and redivided so that the ultimate "blades" (they hardly qualify for the name) are tiny, irregular in outline, and arranged on opposite sides of a midline. A leaf of wild carrot and a leaf of poison hemlock placed side by side are easily told apart, but distinguishing them is not so easy when you don't have both to compare and must trust to memory. One characteristic that is very useful in separating them is presence or absence of hairs. The main stalks of the leaves always are covered with hairs in wild carrot while the leaf stalks of poison hemlock are always perfectly smooth and absolutely hairless.

Most hemlock plants display many conspicuous purple splotches or irregular marks on the main parts of the leaf stalks near where they enter the ground. Poison hemlock and wild carrot both have similar, long, usually unbranched, white-fleshed tap roots, and both have an odor characteristic of the family but distinguishable with practice. Poison hemlock usually lives two years or sometimes more and reproduces readily by seed. It can easily be controlled with herbicides.

Poison hemlock is without doubt the source of the poison with which Socrates was put to death. In classical Greece, plants were not as well distinguished from one another as they are now, and the name by which the Greeks referred to poison hemlock might have

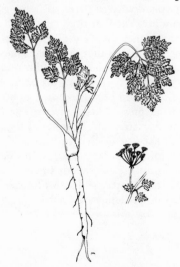

Poison hemlock.
Young plant with single
inflorescence

meant some plant other than *Conium maculatum*. But a very clear description of the symptoms displayed by Socrates before his death has come down to us:

Then Crito made a sign to his slave, who was standing by, and the slave went out, and after some delay returned with the man who was to give the poison, carrying it prepared in a cup. When Socrates saw him, he asked, "You understand these things, my good sir, what have I to do?" "You have only to drink this," he replied, and "to walk about until your legs feel heavy, and then lie down, and it will act of itself." With that he handed the cup to Socrates, who took it quite cheerfully. Socrates, without trembling, and without any change of color of feature, looked up at the man with that fixed glance of his and asked, "What say you to making a libation from this draught? May I, or not?" "We only prepare so much as we think sufficient, Socrates," he answered. "I understand," said Socrates. "But I suppose that I may, and must, pray to the Gods that my journey hence may be prosperous: that is my prayer be it so." With these words he put the cup to his lips and drank the poison quite lively and cheerfully. Till then most of us had been able to control our grief fairly well; but when we saw him drinking, and then the poison finished, we could do so no longer: my tears came first in spite of myself, and I covered my face and wept for myself; it was not for him, but at my own misfortune in losing such a friend. Even before that Crito had been unable to restrain his tears and had gone away; and Apollodorus, who had never once ceased weeping the whole time, burst into a loud cry, and made us one and all break down by his sobbing, and grief, except only Socrates himself. "What are you doing, my friends?" he exclaimed. "I sent away the women chiefly in order that they might not offend in this way; for I have heard that a man should die in silence. So calm yourselves and bear up." When we heard that, we were ashamed, and we ceased from weeping. But he walked about, until he said that his legs were getting heavy, and then he lay down on his back, as he was told. And the man who gave the poison began to examine his feet and legs, from time to time: then he pressed his foot hard, and asked if there was any feeling in it; and Socrates said, "No:" and then his legs, and so higher and higher, and showed us that he was cold and stiff. And Socrates felt himself, and said that when it came to his heart, he should be gone. He was already growing cold about the groin, when he uncovered his face which had been covered, and spoke for the last time. "Crito," he said, "I owe a cock to Asclepius: do not forget to pay it."

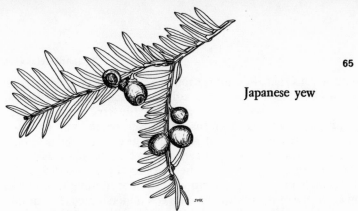

Japanese yew

"It shall be done," replied Crito. "Is there anything else that you wish?" He made no answer to this question; but after a short interval there was a movement, and the man uncovered him, and his eyes were fixed. Then Crito closed his mouth and his eyes.

Such was the end, Eshrecrates, of our friend, a man, I think, who was the wisest and justest, and the best man that I have ever known. [4]

On the basis of these symptoms we have little doubt that the plant used was, in fact, *Conium maculatum*. It contains several alkaloids which are relatively simple in chemical structure among alkaloids, and are chemically related to nicotine. The symptoms they produce are similar to those produced by an overdose of nicotine. These alkaloids work by depressing the function of the central nervous system and bringing on paralysis. Death occurs when the muscles used in breathing become paralyzed.

Ground hemlock, a yew, takes its name from the general resemblance of its foliage to that of the true (nontoxic) hemlock tree. Ground hemlock contains a very potent alkaloid. It grows in dense woods in the eastern half of the United States, from Kentucky northward, and because of its habitat is usually not troublesome. Its close relatives, the Japanese yew and English yew, are among the most common of ornamental shrubs.

All of these species are needle-bearing evergreen shrubs. The needles are relatively short, flat, and broad in comparison with the more familiar needles of pines. Instead of being grouped in bundles as in most needle-bearing evergreens, the needle-leaves of ground hemlock and the yews are organized like the slats of a closed Venetian blind with a stem up the middle. That is, they are inserted oppositely on the leaf-bearing stems, at right angles to the stem in such a manner that they lie flat in the same plane as the stem itself, and

[4] J. W. Harshberger, *Pastoral and Agricultural Botany*. P. Blakiston's Son & Co., Philadelphia, Pennsylvania, 1920.

are so numerous that they almost touch along their long edges.

In these characteristics of shape and orientation, needles of ground hemlock and the yews are like those of the true hemlock tree. Ground hemlock may get to be as much as 5 feet tall and hemlock trees start out as seedlings, so it is possible at certain stages to confuse the two. Fortunately, they can always be told apart with certainty in any stage of growth by the markings of the needles. Each needle of the hemlock tree has two whitish lines running lengthwise, one on each side of the midrib, on its green undersurface. The undersurface of the needles of ground hemlock and the yews lacks these lines and is usually distinctly yellower than the upper surface.

Yews produce bright red berrylike structures instead of cones. Each "berry" has a stony seed at the center. The hard seed is incompletely surrounded by a fleshy, bright red cup. The entire structure is ovoid and not more than three quarters of an inch long. These fruits attract the attention of children, but fortunately the fleshy portion seems to be the least toxic part of the plant. *All other parts* of the plant are very poisonous.

English yew has been judged the most dangerous of the poisonous trees and shrubs in Britain, having caused much loss of life in man and animal. Here in the United States the cases have been fewer, but there is no reason to believe the plant is any less dangerous. Ground hemlock and the ornamental yews contain the same toxic principle, an alkaloid which weakens and eventually stops the heart. If a relatively large amount is eaten, death is sudden with few or no warning symptoms. Sometimes, in the case of animals, parts of the plant can be found in the mouth. If less is eaten, warning symptoms such as trembling and difficulty in breathing may occur before death.

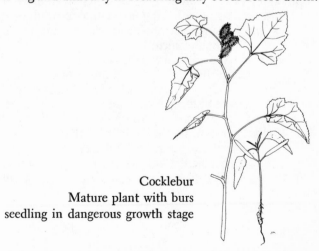

Cocklebur
Mature plant with burs
seedling in dangerous growth stage

In water hemlock it is believed that only the root and young foliage are dangerous. Poison hemlock, on the other hand, contains its poison primarily in the foliage and seeds. In ground hemlock the entire plant is toxic, except perhaps the fleshy part of the "berry," but some evidence suggests that the plant is not equally toxic throughout the year.

Cocklebur is another good example of a plant in which only a certain part—the seed—is toxic. Reserves of carbohydrates and other compounds are normally concentrated in the seeds in most plants. Here they are available for germination and nourishment of the young seedling, a critical stage in the plant's life history. If a plant contains a poisonous compound, this, too, is often concentrated in the seeds even though present in lesser amounts elsewhere in the plant. In cocklebur, the seeds are borne in a hard-surfaced, densely spiny bur, a little less than an inch long, which persists until long after the seeds have germinated within it. The presence and persistence of the bur is fortunate, since neither man nor animals can easily consume the seeds while so protected.

The seedlings are the dangerous stage of the life cycle. Cocklebur seeds germinate best in mud. Seedlings are found along stream banks or about the edges of ponds as the water recedes in spring and summer. They are particularly dangerous when growing about the periphery of farm ponds used for watering livestock. Each seedling first grows two long, straplike leaves, which were already started in the seed. These look something like the first two leaves of a squash plant, but narrower. (See Fig. 30) They are followed soon by leaves of different size and shape from the first two. The seedling loses its toxicity as the later leaves appear, perhaps by dilution of its poison in the expanding tissues of the plant, and is nearly harmless by the time the third and fourth leaves expand. But cocklebur poisoning may occur throughout spring and summer, since seeds remain viable in the soil for months or years and new seedlings appear whenever new mud is exposed as the water line recedes.

Hydroquinone, the poisonous substance produced in the seeds of cocklebur, so far as now known, is not found in any other plant. Its major effects are severe upset of the digestive system accompanied by or followed by general weakness, prostration, and paralysis. Administration of fatty substances such as butter, lard, or linseed oil immediately after the seedlings have been eaten may reduce the severity of poisoning or prevent it.

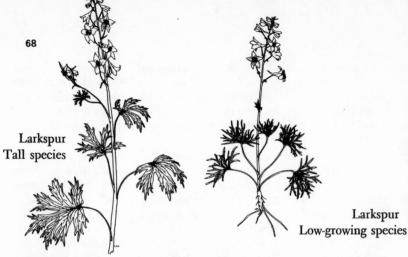

Larkspur
Tall species

Larkspur
Low-growing species

Since the toxic structures of cocklebur and water hemlock are produced only at certain points in the life cycle of the plant, toxicity is seasonally determined for such plants. Larkspurs provide a good example of seasonal toxicity that is not associated with a particular part of the plant. They have been recognized as medicinal and poisonous from classical times, but they are of minor importance as poisonous plants in most countries other than ours. Here, the wild larkspurs of the Western ranges are among the most serious causes of death in cattle. Larkspur was the first plant to be chosen for investigation by the poisonous plants experiment station of the Department of Agriculture. Much of what is known about its toxicity comes as the result of their investigation into its toxicity to range cattle, but this may be expected to apply also to the common garden species.

Larkspurs are generally divided into tall and low-growing species. Both groups contain toxic members. Low-growing species usually appear very early in spring, grow rapidly, flower in spring or early summer, set seed, and die. The life cycle of the tall larkspurs takes place more slowly, and these plants, flowering in the summer and setting seed later, give the best example of seasonal toxicity. Experiments have shown that the youngest growths of tall larkspurs have the highest toxicity on a unit-weight basis. Toxicity decreases as the plant matures. It has been reduced to about one half when the flower buds are formed. After that, toxicity decreases even more rapidly, so that by the time the seeds appear in the seed pods, the toxicity of the foliage is only about one sixteenth that of the first growth. The seeds, however, contain concentrated amounts of the poison.

The poison in larkspurs consists of a group of chemically related, complicated alkaloids. Symptoms of poisoning are primarily nervous in nature. Range cattle are unable to control their bodies, and standing becomes increasingly difficult. Eventually they fall down and cannot regain their feet despite violent attempts to do so, during which they may injure themselves. Death, if it occurs, may be the result of respiratory paralysis, or poisoned cattle may choke to death when they vomit while lying down.

The first part of the digestive system in cattle is the rumen, the first of the "four stomachs." In the rumen, a tremendous sac holding as much as 50 gallons, a controlled fermentation takes place. In this process cellulose, one of the main constituents of plants, is broken down by bacteria and other micro-organisms into simpler forms which may be digested by cattle. Fermentations of this sort have many dangers. One is the production of gas. If a cow cannot belch occasionally, her life is soon in danger. Trapped gasses expand and may burst the rumen. This is called bloat.

Larkspur poisoning often results in bloat. On the hilly or mountainous ranges where larkspurs grow, cattle tend to fall with their heads downhill. In this position the mass of intestines and other organs in the body press forward against the rumen in such a way that belching is difficult or impossible. If the animal cannot turn around or get back on its feet, death from bloat may follow.

Even the sex of plants may influence the degree of toxicity which is developed. In marihuana plants, for example, the sexes are separate. Individual plants bear either only male flowers or only female flowers. Although all parts of both sexes produce some amounts of the active resinoids, the inflorescences of the female plants are by far the most potent source.

Toxicity as related to kind of animal

Larkspur is a poisonous plant to which different kinds of animals react differently. For some reason not yet understood, the alkaloids which it contains are more toxic to cattle than to sheep. Both sheep and cattle eat larkspur quite readily, but sheep are rarely poisoned. They are commonly used on ranges heavily infested with larkspur to help eradicate the plant. Nevertheless, when finally poisoned in experiments, by large doses, sheep displayed about the same symptoms as cattle. The reaction of man and other animals to larkspur has not yet been well established.

Many poisonous plants produce their major toxic effect in the digestive system. Different types of animals differ greatly in the structure and exact function of their digestive systems and so react somewhat differently to this type of poisoning, even though the fundamental nature of the poisoning may be the same. Other differences in the reactions of different animals to the same poison may occur in the biochemical pathways of individual cells. Shellfish poisoning and sleepygrass poisoning are good examples.

Tarweed grows as an annual and is especially common in wheat fields of the Pacific Coast states and Idaho. It is drought resistant and may make good stands in dry years when the wheat does poorly. Its seeds are harvested with the wheat and may be fed to animals either in grain mixtures or in screenings from wheat-cleaning operations. The poison in tarweed causes fundamental damage within the cells of the liver. Horses, swine, and cattle are readily poisoned, but sheep and poultry are singularly resistant. In fact, tarweed seeds may be used in rations for fattening lambs for market.

Another example of the different ways animals respond to the same poison is the reaction produced by very small amounts of scabby barley, that is, barley grain parasitized by a mold named *Gibberella*. The molded grain causes severe vomiting in swine, but cattle seem absolutely immune to it even when fed large quantities. A severe outbreak of poisoning in German swine from exported American barley in 1928 caused the German government to place import requirements for purity on American barley shipped to that country.

Sometimes the sex of an animal influences the reaction to a plant poison. At one time a disease of female swine caused a lot of trouble in the Central States. It appeared after these animals had been fed molded corn forage. This diet caused the genital organs to swell and to prolapse (protrude increasingly from the body). While the disease was not fatal in itself, secondary complications, especially infection, could be if not cleared up quickly. Male animals fed the same ration had little or no sign of poisoning. This unusual type of poisoning was probably due to the formation of a compound in the molded corn that possessed some of the characteristics of a female hormone, or estrogen.

Even the color of the animal may make a difference in determining whether poisoning will take place, and its severity. Photosensitization, discussed in the next chapter, is a disease in which the skin becomes abnormally sensitive to light and undergoes a type of severe sunburn. In order for sunburn to take place, light must penetrate into the skin. Animals with black skin or with a heavy coat of hair usually are not burned even if sensitized by the poisonous compound obtained from the plant. Holstein cows, the common large black and white dairy animals, if sensitized usually are burned only in the areas of white skin.

Large differences exist between man and animals in reaction to potentially dangerous plants. Man vomits easily and can thus relieve himself of poisonous materials. Vomiting often happens spontaneously in cases of poisoning. Water hemlock, for example, would undoubtedly have killed many more human beings than it has except that it commonly induces vomiting. On the other hand, cattle, sheep, goats, and horses cannot vomit effectively.

Most of the differences between man and animals in their reaction to poisonous plants is based upon their different eating habits. Man usually eats some animal products at each meal, so that poisonous plants which might be eaten at the same time are diluted in the digestive system. Moreover a relatively large amount of most plants is required to produce poisoning, and man rarely eats a large amount of any one thing. For man, most of the danger of poisonous plants lies in two areas. First is the natural curiosity of children, which prompts them to experiment indiscriminately with berries, fruits, roots, and other parts of plants—even when they taste bad. Of somewhat lesser importance is the danger in a relatively few plants such as potato and rhubarb which, if not handled properly, may cause trouble. Persons who experiment with wild plants for food, "teas," or homeopathic medicines, of course, are asking for trouble unless they base their usage on authoritative information and reliable identifications.

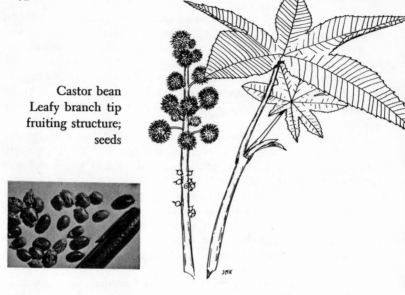

Castor bean
Leafy branch tip
fruiting structure;
seeds

Toxicity as related to growing conditions

The capacity of plants to produce dangerous amounts of hydro-cyanic acid is influenced to a large degree by the nature of the growing season. Plant breeders have developed some strains of sudan grass, which is a sorghum, with a very low cyanide potential. However, cyanide formation varies within wide limits, depending upon how the crop is grown. In general, conditions which retard growth tend to promote cyanide formation. It is also enhanced by the presence of ample soil nitrogen, in which case cyanide content may rise far above the toxic level and warnings may be issued to farmers that immature or stunted sudan grass should be pastured with caution, especially if it is dark green in color. Cyanide formation in arrow grasses which grow in normally moist saline or alkaline soils seems to be similarly influenced by the nature of the growing season.

We do not have enough information to make a statement that some parts of the world or some climates are more dangerous than others because of the poisonous plants they contain. And further-more it probably isn't true even as a generalization.

Toxicity as related to the handling of products from plants

Some plant poisons are easily removed by extracting them in water; others such as the compounds in precatory bean, castor bean, and botulism are inactivated by heat. Castor bean, like the precatory bean, contains a phytotoxin, a protein which is denatured or inactivated by heat. Fortunately, it is not soluble in oil. Hence castor oil technically is not toxic even if personal experience might lead you to believe otherwise. Large amounts of castor oil are used as lubricants in industry and the residue remaining after the oil has been pressed from the castor-bean seeds is nutritious and useful as livestock feed. The phytotoxin it contains must first be inactivated, however, and this is easily accomplished by simply heating the residue.

Cassava is widely cultivated in tropical countries as a source of food. Tubers, somewhat like potatoes, are used in several ways, especially as a source of tapioca. Raw tubers may contain lethal concentrations of cyanide. Natives in several parts of the world independently discovered that either peeling the tubers and heating them, or repeatedly mashing and soaking them in water makes them safe to eat. Both of these processes drive off the cyanide content.

Some persons like to experiment with wild plants as sources of food. Several books give directions on what to try and how to proceed and many of the plants they mention are also listed in books on poisonous plants. Directions for preparing them often include the recommendation to cook in several changes of water. This procedure leeches out or destroys much of the poisonous principle. It is wise to follow this recommendation closely whenever it is encountered and also to try wild plants only in small amounts at first.

Some plants produce more than one type of poisoning. Ergot, for instance, can produce either gangrene or convulsions. The difference in symptoms is probably determined by the amount consumed. Some poisonous plants accumulate nitrate in addition to their normal poison, especially if grown on well-fertilized soils. As we have seen, sudan grass usually is harmless and constitutes desirable forage for livestock. It can, however, form dangerous concentrations of cyanide and sometimes accumulates dangerous concentrations of nitrate.

Rape is a single plant which may produce multiple types of poisoning. Unlike sudan grass or ergot, the fundamental mechanism of rape poisoning is not known. It is widely cultivated as a forage

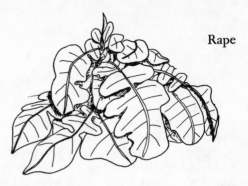

crop in northern latitudes and for its seeds from which an oil is obtained.

Cattle pastured on rape may develop pulmonary emphysema, a commonly fatal disease in which lung tissues become water-logged and less capable of transferring oxygen into and carbon dioxide out of the blood. A second type of poisoning produces results similar to simple overeating. The digestive system quits working and toxic products are formed within it. A third result of rape pasturage is nervous in character. Livestock wander about aimlessly and may become aggressive or even blind. A fourth disease attributed to rape forage is characterized by anemia, jaundice, and blood in the urine. These symptoms indicate damage to the liver. Fifth, uncontrollable hemorrhage within the body has been found in rape-fed poultry. In the sixth place, photosensitization (artificial sunburn) has afflicted swine and other animals and been attributed to the rape in their diet. Finally, rape plants may accumulate dangerous levels of nitrates.

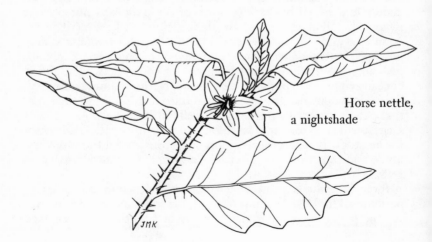

Horse nettle,
a nightshade

4 How Plants Are Toxic

Climbing nightshade
or European bittersweet

Poisonous principles may be classified on the basis of their chemical structure or physiologically (by what they do in the body), and a single poisonous compound may legitimately belong to several different categories of poison. Solanine, the poisonous principle of potato and the nightshades, is at the same time a glycoside, an alkaloid, a saponin, and a steroid.

Nitrogen — necessary but hard to handle

In starvation and malnutrition, deficiency of protein is usually more significant than is deficiency of carbohydrates, which are cheap and relatively easy for man to produce. Usable protein, on the other hand, is much harder to come by in the economy of living processes. Carbohydrates provide energy, but energy alone is useless without protein from which bodily structure is built. The basic chemical difference between carbohydrate and protein is nitrogen, which is present in protein molecules and absent in carbohydrate molecules. This is an oversimplification; there are important structural differences as well, but nitrogen is the key to the matter. Nitrogen, in a form which can be used by plants, is in short supply on this earth and getting it out of the air, where it is plentiful, requires the expenditure of a lot of money and energy.

Biochemically, nitrogen might be likened to a very hot biscuit. It is valuable, but must be handled with precautions. Many compounds of nitrogen with other readily available atoms are quite toxic. One of the most completely understood and best-documented examples of a long evolutionary process is the development of the kidney, from fish to man and bird, to perform the excretion of nitrogen compounds which would be toxic if they were left

Eastern false hellebore

to accumulate in the body. Some compounds containing nitrogen are very poisonous because the body cannot handle them safely even in small amounts.

Alkaloids are such compounds. They were given that name by chemists at the time of their discovery in a previous century because they were like alkalis in many respects. Literally thousands of alkaloids are known and, although they serve no recognized function in plants, they can cause a lot of trouble if they get into animal bodies.

Chemically, alkaloids range from quite simple molecules to very complex ones. Many alkaloids poison one part or another of the highly specialized and evolved nervous system. Thus, an alkaloid often has quite different effects in different animal species, depending on nervous-system development. Certain alkaloids affect nerve function without producing visible injury. Another group of alkaloids causes severe damage within the cells of the liver, usually producing similar symptoms and injuries in different types of animals.

Two members of the lily family, false hellebore and death camas, provide good examples of plants which contain alkaloids acting through the nervous system. False hellebore is a large, striking plant of moist pastures and woods throughout North America. Each plant consists of a single stem, appearing early in spring, usually growing 3 to 6 feet tall. The stem bears many broadly oval, large, stalkless leaves, each 6 to 12 inches long and 3 to 6 inches wide. Each leaf is folded lengthwise like the pleats in a skirt or the bellows in an accordian, and this is the plant's most distinctive characteristic.

False hellebore contains several alkaloids of complex chemical structure. They act on the nervous system in such a way as to cause the small arteries of the body to expand in diameter and the small veins to contract. They also slow the rate and force of the heart's contraction. The over-all result is marked lowering of blood pressure.

The purified alkaloids from false hellebore are sometimes used in medicine to produce this effect. Poisoning by false hellebore is rare because the plant is rarely eaten in sufficient quantity by man (quite a bit is necessary for poisoning to result) and it is usually left strictly alone by animals.

Intensive investigation of a recent discovery concerning the Western false hellebore is under way at the federal poisonous plants research installation in Utah. Western false hellebore has been found responsible for "monkey face" disease of new-born lambs on high mountain ranges in the northern Rockies. The disease takes its name from the fact that a certain number of lambs are born with seriously malformed heads. The nose is usually greatly shortened or absent and the face, therefore, dished in. Sometimes both eyeballs may be

Extreme monkey-face lamb

Courtesy Wayne Binns, U.S. Dept. Agric. Research Serv.

Western false hellebore

Produced malformation
Wayne Binns, ibid

in a single socket in the middle of the forehead, or there may be but a single median eye. Monkey-face lambs cannot nurse successfully and under range conditions usually die shortly after birth. The research at Utah has shown that malformed lambs are produced if pregnant ewes consume moderate amounts of Western false hellebore during a period of a day or two after conception. At other times the plant does not seem to have a toxic effect on the developing embryo. The compound that is responsible for embryo damage is not yet known, but in causing an injury early in the development of the embryo, it is like the condemned drug thalidomide, which produces similar effects in the human female.

The alkaloids in death camas have caused much loss of life in man and among livestock from the Western plains to the Pacific Ocean. This genus includes some 15 species of small perennial herbs which look almost like grasses. The leaves are long and narrow, arising in a clump from the ground. Beneath the ground is an onionlike bulb, but the odor of onion is absent. Each leaf is flat and V-creased along its length. It never has hollow portions. The flowers are well spaced along the upper part of an elongate, erect stem, and each looks like a small white, greenish, or pink lily flower.

Death camas alkaloids are similar in structure to those of false hellebore and their action appears to be similar, but the hypotensive effects are accompanied by digestive upset, with abdominal pain, vomiting, and diarrhea. Death camas is probably responsible for greater loss of life among sheep on the spring ranges of the West than any other plant. American Indians and early settlers were killed by it when they mistook it for edible camas, which it resembles, or for other plants with edible bulbs. Occasional cases still occur.

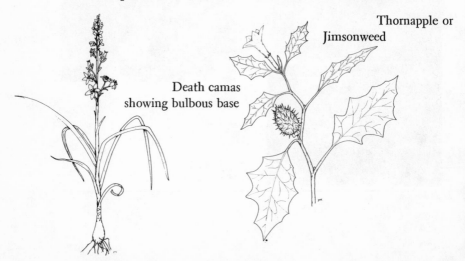

Thornapple or Jimsonweed

Death camas showing bulbous base

Infusions of thornapple are used by some persons to relieve asthma. Occasionally, instead, they cause severe poisoning and death. Thornapple contains alkaloids related to those in belladonna and has a long history of poisoning both man and animals. The plant is a coarse annual weed, which may appear in waste areas, especially in rich soils, throughout much of the United States. Well-developed plants may stand nearly as tall as a man. Leaves are large, coarse, and irregularly margined. The flowers are tubular, several inches long, with spreading lip. They look very much like those of flowering tobacco, only larger, and may be white or purple. The most characteristic part of the plant is its fruit, each one ovoid, greenish, nearly an inch in diameter, and covered in most varieties with stout sharp spines.

Thornapple is dangerous in several ways. Children have been poisoned by sucking the nectar from the base of the flower tubes or by eating the seeds or the fruits which contain them. Both fruits and flowers are large and conspicuous and attract the curiosity of children. Animals sometimes eat the foliage of the plant.

Symptoms are spectacular. The first is a thirst which cannot be satisfied. Vision is disturbed as the result of marked enlargement of the pupils of the eyes, caused by the alkaloids in the plant. Subjects may become excited and delirious or incoherent in speech and apparently insane. They commonly pick at imaginary objects on themselves or in the air. In severe cases the subjects usually experience convulsions and coma. Individual reactions vary greatly. Enlarged pupils persist for many days in patients who have otherwise recovered.

Crotalaria

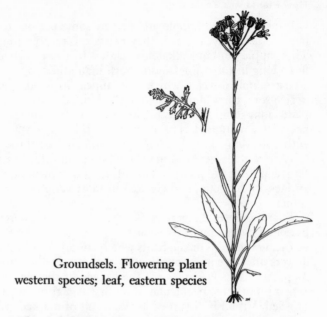

Groundsels. Flowering plant
western species; leaf, eastern species

Crotalaria and groundsel, an inconspicuous weed, are among a small and rather specialized group of plants containing alkaloids which cause severe liver injury. They cause death of functional liver cells, bleeding within the tissues of the liver, rupture of the veins which supply it with blood, and unusual enlargement of some of the liver cells. The last effect seems to be the result of derangement in the normal processes of cell division and some investigators regard the abnormal enlarged cells as cancerous. The liver is a large organ and has great reserve capacity, and a human being can live normally with a large fraction of his liver not functioning at all. Poisons which cause destruction of liver cells usually, therefore, are not rapidly fatal. Instead, as they are destroyed, the functional cells of the liver are replaced slowly with nonfunctional tissue. When the amount of functional tissue in the liver reaches the minimum necessary to sustain the vital processes of that organ, death follows swiftly.

Neither crotalaria nor groundsel has caused poisoning of man in the United States, but both have contributed to economically severe loss of life in livestock particularly in the Northeast and the Western states. Groundsel poisoning of human beings is important in Africa where seeds of the plant occur as contaminants in grain crops. There it is called bread poisoning.

Several species of crotalaria have given promise of agricultural value as soil builders for the exhausted soils of the Southeast. Crotalarias are legumes which, like clovers, can trap atmospheric nitrogen and convert it to a form usable by other plants or animals. They grow well in very poor soils, adding nitrogen and humus to them when plowed under. Several species were brought into the country many years ago by plant explorers of the Department of Agriculture. Unfortunately, two, now widely established, were later found to contain dangerous amounts of liver-damaging alkaloids and have become a serious problem. All later introductions have been first tested for possible toxicity.

Poppy alkaloids are, of course, indispensable in human medicine for relieving pain. Unfortunately some of them are habit-forming and are subject to strict regulation. Opium is the crude mixture of alkaloids from the opium poppy. It is illegal in this country for an unlicensed person to obtain opium poppy plants, transport, grow, possess, or permit them to exist on any land under his control. Before opium poppy was legally restricted in this way, it was a common garden plant, grown for its showy flowers. The poppy most commonly cultivated at present is the Oriental poppy. Poppy alkaloids have been found in this species, but they are usually not the same as the mixture in opium, and control is not needed.

Opium poppy. Flower bud opened flower, mature fruit

Opium poppy. Ripe capsule

Courtesy Prentice-Hall, Inc.

Poppy alkaloids have also been found in some common wild plants such as bloodroot with its bright red sap, and celandine poppy which has bright orange-yellow or yellow sap. Both of these plants are undoubtedly dangerous, but neither has caused real trouble.

Most nitrogen used by the cells of the body goes into protein molecules, which are built of amino acids. A small number of proteins and other amine-bearing molecules are poisonous. Phytotoxins have already been described in connection with precatory-bean poisoning, but another protein molecule which causes trouble is the wayward enzyme. An enzyme is a chemical compound which encourages or speeds up a specific reaction not otherwise involving it. So far as known, only one enzyme in plants causes trouble in animals—the enzyme thiaminase which promotes breakdown of thiamine (vitamin B_1). Thiamine must be present in small amounts in the diet of most animals, since this molecule, absolutely essential in certain fundamental cell reactions, is not formed in the animal body.

Only a few plants contain the troublemaker, thiaminase. Among them are horsetail and bracken fern. When these plants are eaten by simple-stomached animals, the thiaminase in them destroys the thiamine which is present in the diet and prevents the animal from receiving any thiamine from its digestive system. B_1 deficiency results when the bodily reserves of thiamine have been used up, and eventually the animal dies. The same thing would probably happen in the case of man if he ate quantities of either of these common plants without cooking. (Heat destroys thiaminase, which is a protein.)

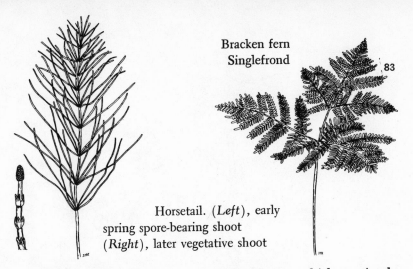

Bracken fern
Singlefrond

Horsetail. (*Left*), early
spring spore-bearing shoot
(*Right*), later vegetative shoot

Both horsetail and bracken have killed horses, which are simple-stomached animals, but neither has produced B_1 deficiency in cattle since these animals are ruminants and can rely on ruminal bacteria for an adequate internal supply of B_1.

Cattle nevertheless have been killed by bracken fern. The unraveling of how the plant kills cattle required extensive research both in the United States and Britain. So far, the poisonous principle has not been identified chemically, but it is a very small molecule and apparently is not a poisonous protein or any other of the usual kinds of poisons. It works slowly on cells of the bone marrow, destroying the living tissue in the hollow cavities of bones. This tissue is very important to continued health because it is the source of red and white blood cells. In bracken poisoning of cattle, the white blood cells decrease to a level where the body has little defense against infection from any small cut or scratch. At the same time, the clotting mechanism of the blood is upset. Cattle poisoned by bracken bleed internally, pass blood with the feces, and sometimes bleed from the eyesockets or nostrils. In healthy cattle, small, normally harmless scratches occur in the intestine from time to time as food passes through. In bracken-poisoned cattle, bleeding comes from these very tiny wounds which otherwise would not be noticed. Bacteria enter the tissues of the body through the same scratches and the body is unable to fight them off. The bacteria multiply within the body tissues and the animal's temperature goes way up. Either bleeding or infection alone would be fatal if uncontrolled.

Usually in medical research, animals are used to test newly developed medicines before they are employed on human beings. In the case of bracken poisoning of cattle the reverse has happened.

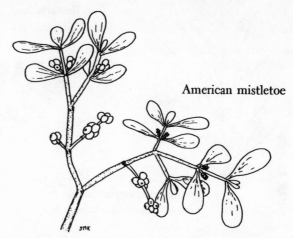

American mistletoe

Overdoses of radiation destroy the cells of the bone marrow just as bracken poisoning does. Much research has gone into discovering effective treatment for radiation damage to the bone marrow in human beings. Researchers were surprised to discover a relation between bracken poisoning and radiation sickness in man as caused by overdoses of X rays or atomic radiation. One compound, batyl alcohol, was found which is able to stimulate to greatly increased activity in forming blood cells whatever healthy tissue may remain in the bone marrow after radiation. This compound has proven remarkably effective in treating bracken-poisoned cattle.

Toxic amines, though not common, contribute to the toxicity of many poisonous mushrooms. Some mistletoes owe their toxicity to this type of compound. Both the American and the European mistletoe, used in Christmas decoration, contain toxic amines. Cattle have been killed by eating wild mistletoe in the oak groves of the Coast Ranges of California.

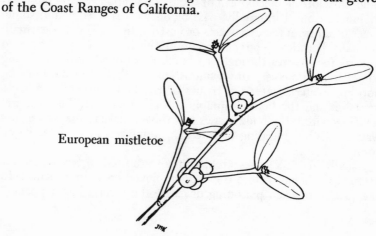

European mistletoe

Recently, medical researchers and biochemists have become interested in the sweet pea, a genus that contains about 100 species, including the common ornamental sweet pea. There are two groups of poisonous species. One group produces paralysis and skeletal deformities resulting in twisted bodies. Bone formation is disturbed in such a way that calcification does not take place properly and cartilage overgrows, much like the bone malformation that takes place in a medical syndrome of humans called premature aging.

The second group of poisonous sweet peas produces excitement and convulsions in experimental animals. Despite these great differences in symptoms, the poisonous compounds in the two groups are chemically related, both amine-bearing, but not identical. Indian pea at one time caused heavy losses of human life in some areas of the world where it was used as food. In this country, danger of sweet-pea poisoning is associated only with species used as livestock feed.

Nitrate is the form of nitrogen most generally available to plants from the soil. Some nitrate is normally present in agricultural soils and the amount is artificially raised by fertilization. When nitrate is plentiful, plants take it up readily into their tissues, some much more easily than others. High concentrations of nitrate in plants may be responsible for a number of different types of poisoning.

The most common is nitrite poisoning. Nitrate itself is mildly poisonous, but as the animal eats the plant it is rapidly converted to nitrite. Nitrite is about ten times more toxic than nitrate. It alters the hemoglobin or red pigment of the blood, so that it is no longer able to carry oxygen, and thus causes asphyxiation at the level of the blood stream. Nitrite poisoning may come from many

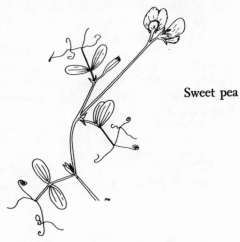

Sweet pea

sources besides plants. Well water of abnormally high nitrate content, lubricants, and fertilizers are examples.

An article in a 1952 issue of *The Cornell Veterinarian* has an intriguing subject—dynamite poisoning of cattle and sheep. One stick of dynamite contains enough nitrate to poison a 450-lb. animal. Apparently some livestock relish, and readily consume, sticks of dynamite left around in removing stumps or rocks from pastures.

Nitrite poisoning from plants is almost exclusively a disease of livestock, since man rarely eats enough of a single species of plant high in nitrate to do him harm. But another disease associated with high nitrate content of forage plants has had more human than livestock victims. It is associated with silage, the fermented forage stored in silos. To make silage, a farmer harvests corn or grass without drying, runs it through a chopper which cuts it up into small pieces, and blows it into the silo. The silo is a large, erect, tanklike, airtight bin, usually two or three stories tall. Conversion of the fresh plant into silage depends on fermentation within the silo, during which lactic acid is produced. Plant materials are preserved by lactic acid which itself is neither distasteful nor harmful to animals.

However, many side fermentations and other reactions may take place at the same time. One involves the production of nitrogen gases from the nitrate in the plants. These gases, chiefly nitrogen dioxide and nitrogen tetroxide, are yellow-brown in color and heavier than air, so they do not evaporate readily from the silo. Instead they may collect in the silo or in the room at its base where the silage is handled for feeding. One or two breaths of the gas at concentrations sometimes reached in such situations result in acute poisoning of man. Tissues of the lung are injured and the lung slowly becomes incapacitated, leading eventually to death. This type of poisoning has been called silo-filler's disease.

Silos sometimes explode and most such explosions are probably the result of gases generated during fermentation. But the suggestion has been made that some particularly vigorous explosions were the result of nitro-cellulose formed in the silage by reaction between its nitrate content and the cellulose of the plants.

Increasingly heavy applications of fertilizers are being used to improve the productivity of agricultural soils. Some agricultural leaders are becoming concerned with the possibility that heavy applications of nitrates to the soil may result in forage crops which are toxic to livestock and research projects have been undertaken to learn more about their potential danger. Members of the amaranth, goosefoot, mustard, composite, and nightshade families tend to take up nitrate more easily than do most other plants. Among crop plants with the tendency to accumulate nitrate easily are celery, oat hay, beets and mangolds, rape, turnip, barley, sweet potato (vines), alfalfa, sudan grass, wheat, and corn. Because they must be consumed in relatively large amounts to produce poisoning, these plants are dangerous to livestock rather than to man.

Plant hormones cause changes in the metabolism or basic biochemistry of a plant, which in turn produce changed patterns of growth. Many of them affect one type of plant differently than another. The herbicide 2,4-D, for example, kills broad-leaved plants by upsetting their growth and metabolism so much that they overgrow and then die. It also upsets biochemical pathways by which nitrate is handled in some plants and may cause nitrate accumulation when it otherwise would not occur. Beet foliage treated with 2,4-D, for example, accumulated much greater levels of nitrate than that of untreated beets, and become dangerous to livestock.

Glycosides

Glycosides are compounds in which one or more substances have been combined with a sugar. Most of them are nontoxic. A few are poisonous as intact molecules while the breakdown products of

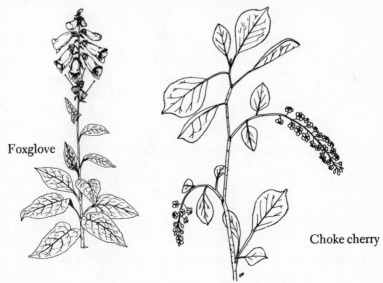

Foxglove

Choke cherry

others are poisonous. Digitalis is a poisonous glycoside. In small amounts it is used medicinally to strengthen the beat of a weakened heart, but in larger amounts, as it might be obtained by animals eating foxglove plants, it is very poisonous.

Cyanogenetic glycosides are nontoxic until the molecule is broken down. Amygdalin is the cyanide-producing glycoside of wild cherries, peaches, almonds, and other members of the rose family. When a plant containing this substance is injured or taken into the digestive system, amygdalin is broken apart into three substances. One is the sugar component; another is cyanide, highly toxic; and the third breakdown product is benzaldehyde.

Cyanide is frequently employed as the lethal substance in murder mysteries, and often the odor of bitter almonds is given as a clue to its presence in the victim. But cyanide itself has no odor; the odor of bitter almonds is that of benzaldehyde. To be correct the source of cyanide in such cases must be from breakdown of amygdalin obtained from one of the plant sources where it occurs. Benzaldehyde itself is not poisonous, but because it occurs in quantitative relationship to cyanide in the amygdalin molecule, the intensity of odor from benzaldehyde is in direct proportion to amygdalin breakdown and hence to release of cyanide.

Often, enough amygdalin is present in bark or leaves of wild cherries, so that the odor of benzaldehyde can easily be detected in

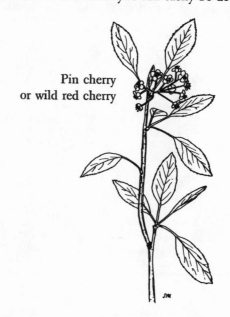

Pin cherry
or wild red cherry

them. Crush the leaves or twist the bark or twigs from a wild cherry tree and place them in a capped bottle. The odor of bitter almonds can usually be noticed after a minute or two, especially if the bottle is kept warm. Sometimes the amount of amygdalin is so great that the characteristic odor is obvious without using a bottle. The odor evaporates rapidly and can be detected in poisoned animals only by immediate examination.

Cyanide poisoning is asphyxiation at the level of the body cells. Each cell requires oxygen, brought to it by the blood, for the chemical burning of food and the release of energy. Oxygen is brought into chemical contact with the material it will burn by a chain of enzymes. Cyanide poisons one of these enzymes and makes it functionless. Therefore, although oxygen is brought to the body cell by the blood stream, and food is available in the cell to be burned, the two cannot get together chemically and the functions of the cell come to a halt. Death of the organism follows. Cells of plants use oxygen in the same manner as cells of animals and are equally susceptible to cyanide poisoning. But cyanide cannot work on these enzymes in plant cells, if it is attached to another substance. Benzaldehyde and sugar are such substances and the *unbroken* cyanide-producing glycoside is harmless to both plants and animals.

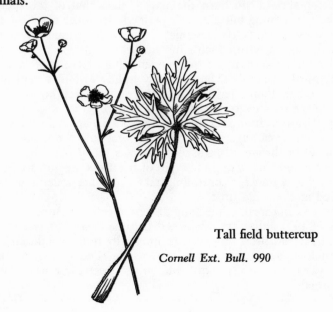

Tall field buttercup

Cornell Ext. Bull. 990

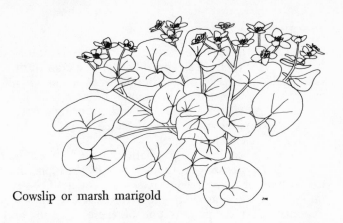

Cowslip or marsh marigold

Many glycosides release a toxic substance when they are broken down by digestion. Goiter-producing compounds in members of the cabbage or mustard family have already been described. These are formed in plants as glycosides. Several buttercups, cowslip, and other members of the buttercup family contain a perfectly harmless glycoside called ranunculin. Ranunculin breaks down very easily, however, to release its nonsugar part, an irritant oily substance called protoanemonin. Protoanemonin causes severe irritation of mouth and digestive system in livestock. The sap of some buttercup species can burn the skin as does that of the spurges. But hay containing buttercups is perfectly harmless since the storing process permits the chemically unstable irritant to change gradually into a form which is not irritant at all.

Mustard oils account for the pungent characteristics of members of the mustard family. They are only mildly irritant except when concentrated; then they can produce quite severe injury to the delicate membranes of the digestive system.

Investigations into poisoning of livestock by spoiled sweetclover hay led, some years ago, to the discovery of a powerful medicine for treatment of thrombosis, the plugging of a blood vessel by a spontaneous blood clot as in some types of heart disease and strokes. A very useful poison for controlling rats and other rodents was discovered at the same time.

A serious outbreak of bleeding disease in cattle occurred in many states in 1921 and, after a while, it became clear that sweetclover hay which had been subjected to unusually moist conditions and had molded, even slightly, was responsible. The haying season of 1921 was exceptionally moist and more sweetclover hay molded than usual.

Molded sweetclover hay somehow reduces the amount of one of the factors needed in the blood for clotting and thus prevents clots from forming. As in bracken poisoning, small cuts or scratches in the walls of the digestive system bleed uncontrollably. Muscle bruises bleed internally and large masses of blood collect beneath the skin. These appear as raised areas on the surface of the body, sometimes becoming several feet in circumference and as much as a foot high. Animals literally bleed to death in their own tissues and large quantities of blood may also be found in the intestines after death. Clotting power decreases steadily over several days or longer, during which animals appear perfectly healthy. But if minor operations such as dehorning are performed on animals in early stages of sweetclover poisoning, bleeding often cannot be stopped and many animals have died in this way.

A lot of people were involved in the hunt for the toxic compound in sweetclover. Toxicity was first associated with the presence in the plant of a bitter compound called coumarin. An ingenious experiment was performed from which it became obvious that under conditions of moisture that lead to mold, two molecules of coumarin combine chemically to form a single molecule of a new substance called dicoumarin. Dicoumarin was then found to be an effective anticoagulant for use in human medicine. This was the principal medicine employed, for example, when President Eisenhower suffered a heart attack while in office.

White sweet clover

Dicoumarin has also been very successful as a rodenticide. Rodents are more susceptible to it than are other animals, so that quantities effective in killing rats are not likely to be sufficient to kill other types of animals. The rodenticide is called "Warfarin" after the initial letters of Wisconsin Alumni Research Foundation, the research laboratory which developed it. One never knows what path will open when new research projects are undertaken. This project, designed originally to learn about the causes and hopefully the control of a disease of cattle, led surprisingly to the discovery of one of man's more useful medicines, to a very effective agricultural chemical, and to excellent financial support for the Wisconsin Alumni Research Foundation.

Saponins — natural detergents

Saponins take their name from the fact that they create a soapy froth or foam when shaken with water. Little is known of the way in which saponins are toxic. They produce intense irritation of the digestive system and the symptoms which that causes, such as vomiting, abdominal pain, and diarrhea, overshadow other effects. If saponins are mixed with blood outside the body, the red blood cells soon burst. This reaction has been suggested as the reason for their toxicity within the body as well, but saponins are not readily absorbed through the wall of the digestive system into the blood.

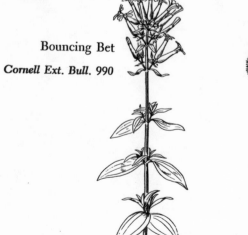

Bouncing Bet

Cornell Ext. Bull. 990

Corn cockle seeds

Because of their saponin content, bouncing Bet and cow cockle have been used by primitive cultures for centuries as a source of a soaplike substance. These common weeds are toxic to livestock, but cases are rare. Saponin-containing plants which have caused great trouble include corn cockle and the tung tree. Corn cockle occurs wild throughout the country, though some strains, selected for large flowers, are grown in flower gardens. It causes trouble when it grows as a weed in fields of winter wheat or rye. Its seeds are roughly the same size as the grains. When farmers have very weedy grain crops they sometimes keep the worst for their own use. In such cases, unless cockle seeds are carefully separated from the grain, it may be toxic when fed to livestock and there could be serious consequences if it were ground for flour for human consumption. Another danger lies in the practice of using the residue, after grains are cleaned, for feeding livestock. When cockle seeds are present in these cleanings, serious poisoning of livestock and poultry may result.

The acreage devoted to raising tung trees in the southeastern United States has increased from year to year in recent decades and now oil squeezed from the large annual crop of tung nuts is used in a variety of industrial products. The residue after extraction of the oil is high in protein and would be valuable livestock

Corn cockle

Tung tree. Twig, mature
fruit, opened fruit, seeds

feed except for the large concentrations of saponin which it contains. Tung-tree foliage also contains saponins and cases of poisoning from both foliage and nuts have become increasingly troublesome. One nut—which may sometimes be eaten by mistake for
Brazil nut—is enough to provoke severe illness in man. Symptoms
appear within a half hour and include vomiting, severe abdominal
pain, and, later, diarrhea. The patient becomes exhausted in a few
hours, and if severely poisoned, may die. Most cases of livestock
poisoning come from prunings or fallen branches. Symptoms are
similar to those in the human being.

Photosensitization — artificial sunburn

Photosensitization is one of the most interesting of diseases of
man or animal. It looks like sunburn, but is usually more severe,
and differs in certain other important respects. Photosensitization
takes place when sunlight reacts with a light-receiving substance, a
pigment in the skin. The skin first is reddened and itches. Next
the capillaries of the circulatory system just beneath the skin become leaky. The fluid in which red and white blood cells are trans-
ported escapes from the injured capillaries and accumulates beneath
the skin, producing a watery swelling called an edema. As the
swelling becomes larger it causes injury within the tissues just beneath the skin and interrupts blood circulation between the skin
and the rest of the body. No longer supplied with blood, the skin
dies and eventually sloughs off.

Photosensitization is primarily a disease of animals, although it
can occur in man under unusual circumstances. In sheep the skin

about the face is usually most injured because there light-screening hair is shortest. The cheeks become swollen, the ears distended and so heavy the animal cannot hold them erect, and the lips and tissues under the chin are swollen and thickened. The fully developed disease in sheep is called "bighead" by the rancher. In severe cases not only does the skin die, dry, and peel off, but parts of the ears and the lips may be lost. Sheep without lips are unable to feed and starve to death. Recently sheared sheep may be "burned" along the back. Black sheep are more resistant than white because the pigmentation in the skin prevents light from reaching the skin capillaries. Cattle are burned in areas where the skin is nonpigmented or lightly pigmented. Photosensitized cattle often have burned or swollen udders and muzzles.

The mechanism by which light makes the tiny blood vessels of the skin become leaky is not known, but the essential feature of photosensitization is the presence of an abnormal pigment in the circulation which causes the reaction with light to take place. Several different pigments can bring this about—among them certain drugs used in human medicine and a pigment chemically related to hemoglobin but found in an unusual congenital disease of cattle. Photosensitization and the source of the photosensitizing pigment is also related to plants.

True sunburn is caused by invisible ultraviolet wave lengths of intense sunlight. Photosensitization, so far as we now know, is caused by wave lengths in the visible portion of the spectrum. Therefore, it can be separated from true sunburn by a simple means: Ordinary window glass absorbs the short ultraviolet wave lengths of light required for sunburn, but not the longer, visible, wave lengths involved in photosensitization. If an experimental animal burns when placed in a greenhouse, it must be photosensitization.

Photosensitization
or "bighead" in sheep

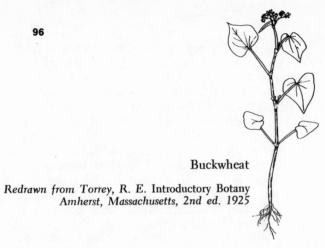

Buckwheat

Redrawn from Torrey, R. E. Introductory Botany
Amherst, Massachusetts, 2nd ed. 1925

Plants cause this condition in two ways. Some plants contain a direct-acting photosensitizing pigment which enters the blood stream and is not excreted or destroyed before it reaches the capillaries of the skin. The animal thereby becomes sensitive to light.

Other plants, the more common, contain a compound which poisons the liver. One of the functions of the liver is the purification and detoxification of blood reaching it from the intestines where digestion breaks down the compounds in food to forms which may be absorbed through the intestinal wall into the blood stream. Many potentially dangerous compounds are changed chemically into harmless forms in the normally functioning liver; others are excreted by the liver into the bile. Many pigments are in the latter category. A liver injured by a plant poison may be unable to eliminate photosensitizing pigments. If not removed, these pigments continue on in the blood stream, reaching the skin where they do their damage.

A major source of pigments reaching the liver from the digestive system is the chlorophyll of plants. One of the digestive breakdown products of chlorophyll is phylloerythrin (literally "leaf-red"). If the injured liver does not remove phylloerythrin from the blood stream, it soon gets into the capillaries of the skin and photosensitization may follow.

In the United States, photosensitization by plants containing a direct-acting photosensitizing pigment is rare and commonly occurs only in buckwheat and St. Johnswort. Buckwheat is a small-grain crop sometimes used for animal feed. Some European countries have had extensive outbreaks of buckwheat photosensitization.

St. Johnswort. Single leaf
shows characteristic pin-point marks

Branch courtesy Cornell Bull. 538, 1963

St. Johnswort is a common weed found throughout the United States. It grows to 3 feet tall, sometimes more, and has clustered branches, the larger of which may become slightly woody. The leaves are less than an inch long with the shape of an elongate oval. Each leaf is dotted with tiny pin-point marks on either surface. These appear black when light is shining on them, but are translucent and yellowish when light is shining through them. The flowers are numerous, yellow, and about an inch in diameter.

The photosensitizing pigments in buckwheat and St. Johnswort are absorbed unchanged through the intestinal wall, pass through the normal liver unchanged, and soon appear in the blood supply of the skin. Photosensitization by these plants, therefore, requires only plant, light-skinned animal, and light.

Sacahuista or beargrass

Historically photosensitization involving liver injury has been associated with a limited number of plants including lechuguilla, sacahuiste, horsebrush, puncture vine, and lantana. All but the last are plants of Western range lands. Horsebrush is the most dangerous among them and has produced bighead in tens of thousands of sheep. An interesting sidelight on poisoning by sacahuiste is that this plant has hard, almost needlelike leaves which are not relished and are rarely eaten by livestock. The succulent buds, blooms, and fruits, however, are sometimes consumed in quantity. These parts contain no chlorophyll. Photosensitization does not occur from sacahuiste unless the diet contains a source of chlorophyll. The liver injury caused by these plants is serious in itself and may cause death whether or not accompanied by photosensitization.

Lantana is a common ornamental plant grown outdoors in the South and as a pot plant elsewhere. The liver toxin in lantana is related chemically to some of the more complex alkaloids. Lantana is particularly dangerous to livestock because clippings and prunings may be thrown where animals have access to them. A number of cases of lantana poisoning in children are on record. Instead of photosensitization, these are characterized by extreme muscular weakness and circulatory collapse. Less severe cases have displayed signs mainly of gastrointestinal irritation.

Lantana

Horsebrush

Oxalates

Oxalic acid is only weakly acid and, except in most concentrated form, does not burn living tissue; yet it is highly toxic due to the fact that calcium and oxalic acid precipitate to form calcium oxalate which is almost completely insoluble. The balance between calcium and other minerals dissolved in blood is very important to the proper functioning of an organism. Proper function of the nerves, especially, and the ability of the blood to form a clot depend on this balance. If oxalic acid appears in the blood stream, calcium precipitates with it and blood mineral balance is seriously altered.

Results of calcium oxalate precipitation reach further than this upset in mineral balance, important as it may be. Calcium oxalate is a foreign substance in the blood stream and it collects in the kidneys. Small crystals, much like rock salt, form in the excreting tubules of the kidney and increase in size as more material is added to them. Eventually they completely plug the excreting tubule and may even burst it. Either result is serious. If the normal poisons in the blood, especially the waste nitrogenous compounds, are not removed steadily from the body by properly functioning kidneys, they accumulate in the blood, and uremic poisoning results. Oxalate poisoning, then, is a combination of effects of the imbalance of blood minerals and plugging of kidney tubules. Symptoms appear in 2 to 6 hours and consist of depression, difficulty in breathing, prostration, coma, and death.

Most of the really dangerous oxalate-bearing plants are range vegetation in the grazing country of the Southwest. These include especially halogeton and greasewood, both of which have been responsible for extensive losses in flocks of range sheep, sometimes more than 500 animals at one time. Halogeton plants have been found in which oxalates constituted 34.5 per cent of the dry weight!

The whole story of the halogeton plant is now known, from its introduction from Russia in the 1930's, to the discovery of its toxicity, the attempt to control its spread, and its current distribution throughout large areas of several Western states. Halogeton is well adapted to life on alkaline desert soils such as are found in many of our Western states. It is capable of populating the most barren, dry lands, gathering sufficient moisture for successful growth and spread. Up to a third of the weight of the plant may consist of oxalate salts and the plant is therefore highly toxic.

Halogeton was first discovered in Nevada in 1934. It was able to populate soils where no other plants had succeeded in establishing themselves and moisture could be squeezed out of its fleshy leaves even under the dryest conditions. Although suspicious losses of flocks of sheep began to occur in the later 1930's, during the next decade halogeton spread faster than the knowledge of its toxicity in spite of the published experiments by the Nevada Experiment Station. As a result, some spectacular losses took place. For example, in Idaho alone, 750 and 1,620 sheep were lost in one day from single flocks. Sheepmen were put out of business; and in 1949 scare headlines were appearing in Western newspapers. Concern soon reached

Halogeton. Young plant and branch with mature winged fruit

Halogeton. Spreading to new territory as wind from passing vehicles carries seeds

the national level (see *Life* Magazine, January 15, 1951), and emergency legislation placed state and federal funds behind a program of control. There were many who seriously believed that the sheep industry of western United States would be ruined by halogeton.

The immediate reaction was to eliminate this annual plant from the West. Much effort was expended in eradicating it from large areas of range. But not enough attention was given to the plant's ability to reproduce by seed. It has been estimated that one halogeton plant produces as many as 50,000 seeds and that an acre of halogeton sets some 500 lbs. of seed. In depressions, or behind windbreaks, seeds accumulate by the handful. Leaving only 1 per cent of the plants alive provides ample seeds to re-establish the population the next year.

Seed is easily spread by animals, by moving automobiles or trains, in shipments of wool, on earth-moving equipment, and in myriad other ways impossible to control.

Early efforts to eradicate or control the spread of halogeton consisted of plowing or spraying hundreds of acres of range. Although most of the halogeton was killed in the first year, so were most of the desirable range plants that had been there, leaving the treated land absolutely bare. The next year, halogeton seeds remaining in the soil germinated in great number until the barren land produced a denser stand of halogeton than before. Attempts to kill halogeton in restricted areas followed by seeding with desirable range plants were unsatisfactory. Seeding the dry soils where halogeton is found is usually unsuccessful and the unwanted plant comes back quickly.

But the sheep industry of the West has not been destroyed and spectacular losses of sheep from halogeton no longer occur. In this, as in almost all cases of danger from wild plants to livestock, control is effected not by destroying the plant—usually impossible—but by farsighted practices of animal husbandry and intelligent use of agricultural lands. We learn to live with our poisonous plants problems now, just as we did in colonial days.

Smaller amounts of oxalates—but still enough to make them potentially dangerous—are contained in a number of food plants. Rhubarb is the prime example. The familiar rhubarb of the grocery store is the stalk of the leaf. Both leaf stalk and leaf blade are sour to the taste, due to their acid content. The stalk contains mostly malic acid, which is quite harmless. The acidity of the blade, however, is chiefly due to the presence of citric and oxalic acids, the latter present in the blade in sufficient amount to be dangerous.

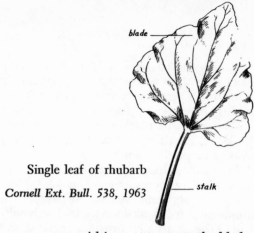

Single leaf of rhubarb

Cornell Ext. Bull. 538, 1963

Every now and then some person wishing not to waste the blades of rhubarb, prepares them for the table. Occasional deaths of human beings have followed such experimentation. Even more disastrous was an epidemic of poisoning which occurred in Britain during the First World War. In an effort to conserve food, a government source recommended that rhubarb blades be eaten instead of thrown away. Despite prompt retraction and great resulting publicity, many cases of severe poisoning and death occurred.

Rhubarb blades should always be discarded and never used as human food. Putting them in garbage for commercial disposal is harmless because by the time the garbage reaches swine, if it does, the rhubarb will have been well mixed with other garbage and

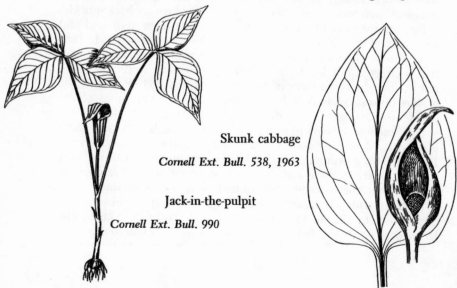

Skunk cabbage

Cornell Ext. Bull. 538, 1963

Jack-in-the-pulpit

Cornell Ext. Bull. 990

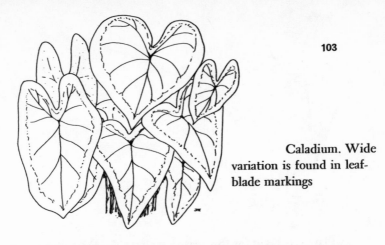

Caladium. Wide variation is found in leaf-blade markings

thereby diluted beyond the point of danger. Rhubarb blades should be kept out of garbage intended for home-grown pigs.

The amount of oxalate in a garden plant depends in part on the conditions under which it has grown. Occasionally, potentially dangerous amounts of oxalates have been detected in beets, purslane, sorrels, Russian thistle, and other plants. These plants are only rarely dangerous to livestock, probably never to man.

Spinach, as previously mentioned, contains moderate levels of oxalic acid, though not enough to poison directly. However, nutritionists have found that, in experimental animals *on a diet barely meeting minimal calcium requirements,* the oxalate in spinach precipitated and made unavailable enough of the dietary calcium to cause definite calcium deficiency and eventual death.

Some plants contain crystals of calcium oxalate which, if eaten, remain largely undissolved during passage through the digestive tract and are excreted. Being unabsorbed by the blood stream, they cannot produce oxalate poisoning as described above. But crystals of calcium oxalate cause trouble of another kind as anyone who has bitten into the root of a jack-in-the-pulpit plant or dumbcane can testify. The sharp-pointed oxalate crystals in these plants, even though microscopic in size, penetrate the tender tissues of the mouth and tongue. The intense burning which results is probably due in part to mechanical and in part to chemical irritation. Dumbcane gets its common name from the fact that intense irritation of the mouth and throat usually prevents a person from talking for a while. Some think practical jokes with these plants are funny, but the truth is that more than one person has lost his life when tissues about the back of the tongue swelled up and blocked breathing as a result of taking a mouthful.

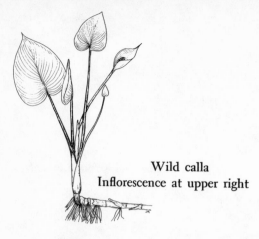

Wild calla
Inflorescence at upper right

Plants to avoid for this reason include also the following: alocasia, caladium, wild calla, elephant's-ear, some philodendrons, and skunk cabbage. Most plants with irritant crystals of calcium oxalate are members of the arum family, a major source of ornamental pot plants.

Resinoids — chemical leftovers

Before present techniques and equipment were available, chemists performed analyses of plant materials by repeated extraction followed by purification. Substances remaining were termed resinoids and sometimes the resinoid fraction was responsible for the toxicity of the plant.

The toxic principle of the poisonous members of the heath family is a resinoid of as-yet-unknown structure. Marihuana is a plant in

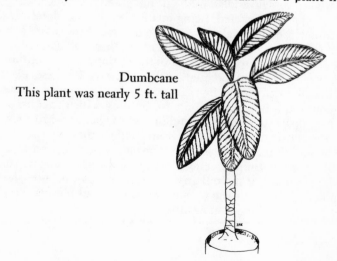

Dumbcane
This plant was nearly 5 ft. tall

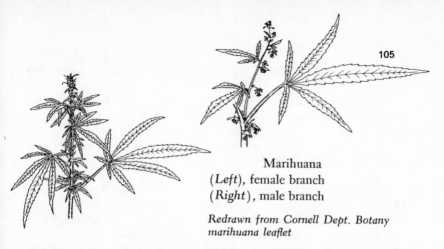

Marihuana
(*Left*), female branch
(*Right*), male branch

Redrawn from Cornell Dept. Botany marihuana leaflet

which the poisonous principle, though now known chemically, is still commonly called a resinoid.

Marihuana is narcotic. It is only on the verge of being habit-forming itself, but persons who start using marihuana usually soon turn to stronger habit-forming drugs, such as the opium derivatives. The plant, parts of the plant, and products made from it, intended for illegal narcotic use, have been given nearly a hundred common names and are all subject to strict federal and state legislation.

Control has been particularly difficult for two reasons. In the first place the marihuana plant is the source of hemp fibers used in making rope. Its seeds are a common constituent of bird-seed mixtures and they also yield a useful oil. Commercial cultivation of the plant ceased in the United States in 1955, but by that time it had become widely distributed throughout the country as a weed. In some alluvial bottom lands along the Mississippi and Missouri rivers it has covered thousands of acres.

Marihuana is variable in its appearance as well as in its ability to form narcotic resinoid. The plants are coarse annual herbs, 3 to 6 feet tall, reproducing by seeds. Hemp seeds in bird-feed mixtures now must be sterilized before use so they are no longer capable of spreading the plant. The most distinctive part of the much-branched plant is the leaf. Leaves vary greatly in size, depending on position on the plant, the larger on the lower portions. Each has a long stalk and 5 to 7 long narrow leaflets arranged at the tip of it like the fingers of a hand. Each leaflet is coarsely toothed along its margins and tapers at the tip. The teeth are broad, relatively blunt, and about equal in size.

Unfortunately, sulfur cinquefoil, a common weed, has similar leaves. Cinquefoil is usually a smaller plant, unbranched or less branched, and has a single relatively large yellow flower at the tip of each stem.

Marihuana plants are either male or female. In both sexes the flowers are very small, green or greenish white, and grouped in inflorescences. Each male inflorescence is an open cluster of thousands of flowers borne like a tassel at the tip of each branch. The female flowers form much smaller clusters among the leaves along the length of the stem.

The resinoid is contained in all parts of the plant but is particularly concentrated in the mature inflorescences of the female plant. The amount of resinoid found in any part varies tremendously and is dependent on variety, geographical location, and growing season. Its production is greater in warmer climates. The resinoid may be brought into the human body in a number of ways. Use of potent plants is as simple as mixing leaf fragments with tobacco and smoking the mixture.

The structure of the narcotic compound has been worked out only in recent years but its effect on man has been known for at least two thousand years. The reaction of an individual to the drug is relatively unpredictable, but commonly one experiences, first, a period of happiness, elation, and increased awareness of sensations and stimulations. This is followed by a period of hallucination and obvious mental confusion. If the dose is large enough, the marihuana user experiences a third period of depression and comalike sleep. Withdrawal symptoms in long-time users are mild or absent, but continued use of the plant leads most persons to look for a source of stronger "kicks."

Animals are smarter. Despite the common occurrence of the plant in some parts of the world, cases of marihuana poisoning in animals are rare.

"Mother" earth

Man depends on the earth for his nourishment, though plants are the intermediaries. The thin crust of soil which covers only a small fraction of the surface of our planet contains the necessary minerals and water for plant growth and is structured in a way that allows plants to obtain from it the raw materials for their growth. Relationships of plants and soil are remarkable in complexity and effectiveness. There has been vast research aimed at discovering the nature of these relationships and learning how to manipulate them to our advantage. The astonishing agricultural bounty

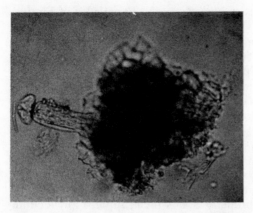

Marihuana
Greatly enlarged
photomicrograph
of glandular structure
which produces narcotic

of our country is the result. But sometimes "mother" earth plays tricks on us. Something goes wrong, and plants are no longer wholesome, even though they apparently are unchanged. Natural tricks of this sort are rare, but they are particularly troublesome because they must be discovered the hard way—by sickness and loss of life.

As we have seen, soils which bear low concentrations of selenium may supply that element to certain accumulating plants and others may passively take up dangerous amounts of selenium from soils where it is abundant. Selenium, in many of its characteristics, is chemically similar to sulfur, which is used in some of the key molecules of living organisms. Although not yet conclusively established, evidence suggests that selenium is sometimes confused with sulfur, and taken into vital molecules of the body, where by making the molecule slightly different, it jams the biochemical machinery.

Selenium offers the most serious example of "mother" earth having become dangerous, but there are other soils in which other elements occur to excess. Usually they pose no problem to the health of man or animals because edible plants cannot grow there. One exception is the presence of large amounts of molybdenum in some soils. Molybdenum poisoning was first discovered in England, where it is called teartness, and it has since been found in many other countries. Molybdenum is especially troublesome in New Zealand and an extensive research program has been undertaken there. In this hemisphere, soils with dangerously high molybdenum content occur in scattered and strictly limited areas in the San Joaquin Valley of California, in valleys at the edges of the

Sierra Nevada Mountains of Nevada, in the Everglades of Florida, and in Canada.

The strong accumulatory power some plants have for soil selenium has not been found in the relationship of plants with molybdenum. However, poorly drained alkaline soils are more apt to be dangerous in this respect than others. Of agricultural forage crops, legumes, consistently take up more molybdenum than grasses. Some soils which yield toxic legumes may be used safely for grass crops.

Molybdenum and copper are antagonistic in animal nutrition and many symptoms and injuries found in molybdenum poisoning can be explained as a copper deficiency. Molybdenum somehow substitutes for copper in the animal's body, but the resulting compounds cannot function properly. Soils which support molybdenum toxicity are usually abnormally low in copper. Copper compounds can often be effectively administered to livestock to prevent poisoning.

Molybdenum poisoning takes a long time to develop. It is found in livestock which have been pastured on or fed continuously from dangerous fields. Symptoms include emaciation, persistent diarrhea, stiffness, and change in color of the coat. The last is sometimes so striking that it might be possible to diagnose molybdenum poisoning in cattle from a helicopter.

Too much copper in the diet is as troublesome as too little. Excessive copper in soils may cause copper poisoning through the vegetation growing on them, but this poisoning is very rare. Forage from certain soils, however, promotes copper accumulation in animals and eventual development of symptoms of copper poisoning and even death.

Copper poisoning may occur as the result of spray programs in orchards. Bordeaux mixture, which contains copper sulphate, was the first fungicide developed and it has served for many decades to protect apple orchards and other fruits against fungus infections. Use of Bordeaux mixture in large amounts year after year in the same orchard could eventually build up the copper content of the soil to the point where trouble can result if animals are pastured under the trees, or if the land is used for forage crops immediately after the trees are removed. However, despite the thousands of acres which have been treated in this way, actual poisoning is practically nonexistent. With the advent of newer organic fungicides, less copper sulfate is currently employed and the potential problem should disappear.

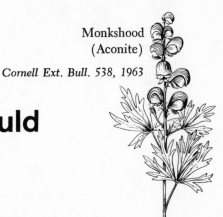

Monkshood
(Aconite)

Cornell Ext. Bull. 538, 1963

5
Plants
Everyone Should
Recognize As
Dangerous

Everyone should be able to recognize as dangerous many of the plants used to illustrate earlier topics in this book. In this section several other equally dangerous and important garden and wild plants are described.

Garden plants

Garden aconite and Christmas rose belong to the buttercup family. Aconite is closely related to larkspur which it resembles in color and general appearance. They can be told apart by the presence of a spur projecting to the rear in a larkspur blossom. People have died after eating small amounts of garden aconite. Christmas rose or true hellebore has been considered poisonous since the time of Dioscorides. Perhaps its evil reputation has kept people away from it, since cases of poisoning in man have been rarely recorded. Its poison remains unknown.

Bleeding heart of the perennial garden has several wild relatives such as Dutchman's breeches, squirrel corn, and Western bleeding heart. All contain alkaloids related to those in some of the poppies. The wild species have been responsible for occasionally severe loss of livestock in the early spring upland wooded pastures of the

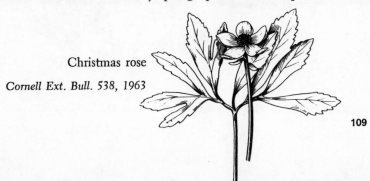

Christmas rose

Cornell Ext. Bull. 538, 1963

109

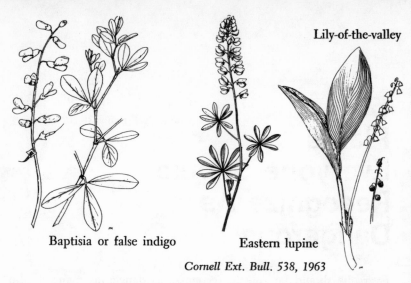

Lily-of-the-valley

Baptisia or false indigo   Eastern lupine

Cornell Ext. Bull. 538, 1963

East and Central states. The cultivated species does not seem to have caused poisoning of livestock and none of the species has poisoned man as far as is known. Nevertheless the demonstrated presence of toxic alkaloids in all of them and the record of toxicity of some for livestock should be ample warning that the garden species may be dangerous.

Baptisia or false indigo and lupine are a pair of look-alikes. Both have palmately organized leaflets and bear erect terminal inflorescences of blue flowers. Neither has been particularly troublesome, but baptisia is known to contain active poisonous principles and the common garden lupine contains some of the same alkaloids found in range lupines. Some range lupines are among the half dozen most troublesome poisonous plants of certain Western states. Losses of over 1,000 animals in some flocks of sheep have been traced to lupine poisoning, though other species of range lupine seem perfectly harmless and are regularly used as forage for sheep.

Dutchman's breeches

Cornell Ext. Bull. 990

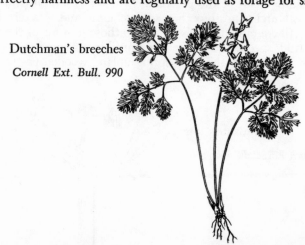

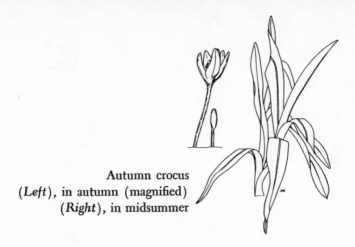

Autumn crocus
(*Left*), in autumn (magnified)
(*Right*), in midsummer

Yellow oleander, or be-still tree as it is sometimes called, and lily-of-the-valley might seem to have little in common. Both are used as ornamentals. The former is a large shrub or small tree of the dogbane family and is limited in distribution to Florida and Hawaii. Lily-of-the-valley is a small perennial herb of the lily family which has been commonly planted in gardens for generations. As unlike as they are, both contain cardioactive glycosides like those of digitalis. Like digitalis, these plants are poisonous if consumed in moderate amount, though lily-of-the-valley is the less dangerous of the two. This may be due to the fact that it is less potent or more distasteful. Be-still tree, on the other hand, has enough potency to kill easily, hence its common name. On Oahu, be-still tree is rated as the most frequent source of serious or lethal poisoning in man. The nuts are usually involved and one or two may be fatal. Many human deaths have also resulted from misuse of this plant or decoctions of it as medicine among native populations in some countries.

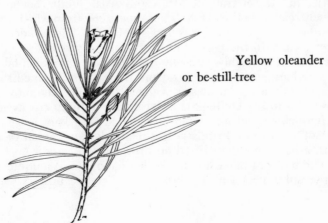

Yellow oleander
or be-still-tree

Star-of-Bethlehem

The lily and amaryllid families which supply us with many of our choicest ornamental plants also contain many toxic members, and some of the ornamentals are among them. Toxic alkaloids are found in lilies such as autumn crocus, star-of-Bethlehem, garden hyacinth, glory or climbing lily and squill. Autumn crocus is the source of colchicine, an alkaloid which has the unusual ability to interfere with the process of cell division. It has been employed by plant breeders and horticulturists to produce mutant and polyploid plants of interest to the gardener. Star-of-Bethlehem is a bulbous plant which has escaped from cultivation in some places. The bulbs are the dangerous part. They have caused deaths among children, and livestock also have been killed by bulbs from plants naturalized in pastures and fields. Bulbs may be brought to the surface by frost heaving, plowing, or the rooting about of hogs. Climbing lily is known to contain an alkaloid similar to colchicine and has caused deaths among human beings in its native habitat of tropical Africa and Asia. Squill (*Scilla spp.*) is closely related to the plant *Urginea maritima* from which red squill powder, used for killing rodents, is obtained. The powder owes its effectiveness to the presence of cardioactive glycosides and to the fact that it is readily eaten by rodents. Some ornamental species of squill are known to be toxic and it has been assumed that they also contain a similar poison. Among these lilies, the most dangerous so far in the United States have been autumn crocus and star-of-Bethlehem, but all should be handled with knowledge of their potential danger. (Fritillaria is a relatively rare garden or pot lily with a bad reputation based on little real evidence.)

The bulbs of narcissus, also called daffodil and jonquil, contain active substances which cause severe digestive upset when eaten

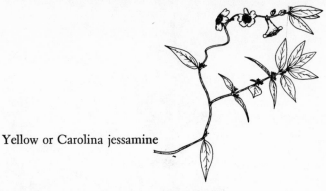

Yellow or Carolina jessamine

even in small amounts. Bulbs of narcissus, snowdrop, and hyacinth were found to possess toxicity when they were fed to livestock facing starvation in the Netherlands during the last war. The first two are members of the amaryllis family. Many members of this family contain alkaloids and some, such as amaryllis, crinum lilies, blood lily, and nerine have proven toxic to livestock in other parts of the world.

Yellow or Carolina jessamine is a showy, woody, evergreen vine with clear yellow, fragrant, trumpet-shaped flowers, about one inch long, appearing in late winter or early spring. It grows in many wild habitats of the Coastal Plain and lower hills from Virginia to Texas. Its nectar apparently contains alkaloids related to strychnine such as are found in the plant itself. Children have been poisoned by sucking nectar from the flowers. Honey bees have also been poisoned by it, and honey made from it is poisonous as well.

Poinciana or bird of paradise is a showy shrub, or small tree, cultivated outdoors in the Gulf Coast states westward; elsewhere as a pot plant. Its clustered large yellow flowers are like those of

Wild iris or blue flag

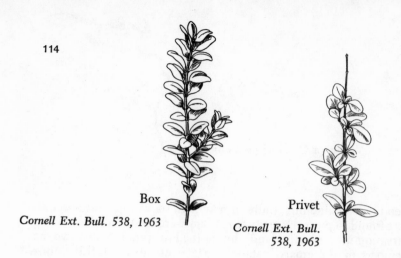

Box

Cornell Ext. Bull. 538, 1963

Privet

*Cornell Ext. Bull.
538, 1963*

sweet pea and ripen into similar leguminous pods. The pods, up to ¾ inch wide and 4 inches long, have caused severe poisoning in children. Like wisteria to which it is related, poinciana causes severe digestive upset, accompanied by vomiting and profuse diarrhea.

Wild and cultivated irises contain an irritant substance in the leaves and particularly in the fleshy underground rhizome. Severe digestive upset follows eating moderate amounts. Wild irises are easily recognized in flower, but the non-flowering plant closely resembles a number of others such as cattail or sweet flag. Possession of both long, linear, erect, parallel-veined, sharp-pointed, two-ranked leaves, and thick, fleshy, mostly horizontal underground rhizomes serves to separate iris from the others. Children should be warned not to eat the fleshy portions of garden or wild irises.

Hedge plants

Hedge plants seem to have more than their share of poisonous kinds. Yew, box, privet, and hydrangea all are dangerous, some more than others. Box is the most important as a poisonous plant. It contains alkaloids and some other active compounds. Many kinds of animals have been killed by clippings from box hedges or single specimen plants. Apparently only a small amount of leaves is required to produce death. Symptoms and injuries are those associated with irritation in the digestive system, often severe enough to result in blood passed with the feces. Hydrangea, both ornamental and wild, may contain cyanide and has killed or severely poisoned

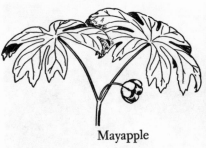

Mayapple

Cornell Ext. Bull. 538, 1963

livestock. But the symptoms and injuries of some well-described cases are not those usually associated with cyanide poisoning. No explanation for this difference is known. Poisoning by privet is rare, but some cases in children have been reported. Poisoning is like that from box.

Wild plants to be recognized as dangerous

None of the plants in this section possesses extreme toxicity. But because each is common or attractive for one reason or another, and dangerous to some degree, they require attention.

Mayapple stands out to the eye among other plants and is a common plant of roadsides, open woods, and wet meadows throughout most of North America. Each plant bears either one or two leaves and consists of little else. The leaves are erect, ½ to 1½ ft. tall, long-stalked, and broad-bladed. Each blade is held more or less horizontally at right angles to the stalk, like an umbrella. Only plants with two leaves produce flowers. A single, nodding, white flower terminates a short stem which grows from the point where the two leaves diverge. It ripens into an ovoid, yellow, irregularly blotched, fleshy fruit, 1 to 2 inches long. This is the "mayapple," the source of its common name. American Indians used mayapple root to "cure" a variety of ailments, and they were soon copied in this by the early settlers. The plant, especially the fleshy underground portion, yields a resinoid with violent cathartic properties. In recent decades, a compound isolated from the resinous fraction has shown marked selective ability to kill certain types of cells and has been put to use in treating some kinds of undesired growths on the human body. The ripe "apple" is often consumed by children. Occasionally, purging may result, but the fruit seems to be the least toxic part of the plant. Those who experiment should be aware of its potential danger.

(*Left*), Pokeweed. (*Right*), Scrub oak

Moonseed is dangerous chiefly because it can be confused with wild grape. Although the vines, the leaves, the "grapes" and the habitat all are similar, one can be told from the other by the following two characteristics. The leaf in grape has 20 or more large teeth around its edge, and each tooth comes to a point; the leaf in moonseed has 10 or fewer, and broader, unpointed lobes. The seeds in grape are numerous and ovoid, while in moonseed only a single, large, crescent-shaped seed is found in each "grape." Grape and moonseed can be told apart by taste, also. But children, sometimes, are not stopped by the difference in taste and poisonings have occurred. Fortunately moonseed, native to eastern North America, is a rare plant, or poisonings might be more frequent. The poisonous compound is unknown.

It seems most everyone has heard of pokeweed (also called scoke, garget, pigeonberry and other common names), but what they have heard varies considerably. Pokeweed is a plant easily remembered when seen in fruit, or by anyone who has tried to dig up its tremendous tap root. It grows commonly in disturbed soils, especially those that are rich and moist, throughout the eastern United States and southeastern Canada. It is especially common in barnyards. The plant reaches a height of 10 feet under favorable conditions. The much-branched stems are thick, and purple-red or green in color. They die back to the ground each winter. The leaves are good-sized and numerous. The inflorescences of small white or greenish flowers are relatively inconspicuous at the tips of the stems, but each flower ripens into a large, shiny purple berry with inky juice. The drooping conical clusters of purple berries on conspicuously red inflorescence stems are very showy and attractive. The tap root lives through the winter and increases in size from year to year. In old plants it may have the thickness of a human thigh. Pokeweed contains more than one physiologically active compound of as yet undetermined identity. Like mayapple, pokeweed was used as a source of medicine by the Indians and early settlers. The root is the most active part. Poisoning from the plant itself is rare, but overdoses of medicines made from it at one time caused many cases of poisoning. The berries are the most attractive part of the plant, and fortunately, the least toxic. They are harmless in the manner and amounts usually used, but death in man from eating them has occasionally been reported.

Several common trees are poisonous. They include some, if not all, species of oak, black locust, horsechestnut, and buckeye.

Oaks are probably never dangerous to human beings but have caused extensive loss of life in livestock. This difference is due to the fact that a large amount of oak must be consumed over an extended period of time to produce symptoms. Oak poisoning is one of the very few types of plant poisoning which may be successfully diagnosed on the basis of injury alone. Oak injures the kidneys in a way unlike that caused by any other poison or disease. An experienced veterinary pathologist should be able to diagnose a case of oak poisoning merely by examining kidney sections from the subject. Oak poisoning in animals is usually the result of browsing on foliage of scrub oaks or on trees which have been felled. Poisoning from acorns is rare. It sometimes occurs in swine, when they have been allowed to feed on large quantities of acorns over several days or weeks. The poisonous compound in oak is unknown.

Black locust is more dangerous, both to animals and man, although fewer animals have been poisoned by it than by oak. It is more dangerous because considerably less is needed for fatal results. Black locust is a common tree, native to eastern United States and Canada. Following recommendations of state and federal agricultural agencies, many farmers have planted black locust to replace chestnut as a source of decay-resistant fence posts, since chestnut has become nearly extinct from the effects of the uncontrollable chestnut blight which appeared in the 1920's and 1930's.

A number of toxic compounds have been isolated from bark and leaves of black locust. There is a lot of confusion in the names and characterizations which have been applied to them. In any event, relatively small amounts of the bark, foliage, or young sprouts bring on symptoms of dullness and depression, vomiting, diarrhea, weakened pulse, and coldness of arms and legs. These symptoms may be divided into two types, one caused by irritation of the

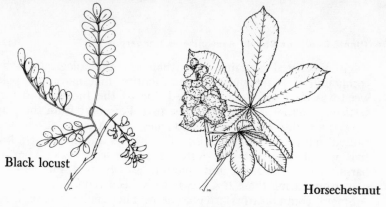

Black locust

Horsechestnut

digestive system and the other probably caused by a reaction between the poison and the nervous system. Poisoning of horses was formerly more frequent when they were more numerous. They were often tethered unknowingly to a locust tree and poisoned when they browsed the bark. Cattle have been poisoned by eating young sprouts of black locust when pastured on cut-over lands. One of the most notorious cases of mass poisoning of human beings occurred in 1887. It happened at the Brooklyn Orphan Asylum and 32 boys were involved. They had eaten bark from black locust fence posts which had been stripped in the orphanage yard. Following heroic efforts by physicians, all recovered. Black locust seeds are produced in long, hanging pods which look something like large, flat pea pods. The seeds may be toxic to children, according to one report, and should be avoided.

Wild buckeyes and the ornamental horsechestnut are closely related. All are woody shrubs or trees whose leaves are composed of 5 to 7 leaflets, palmately arranged. All species can be recognized by the seed which is a large, shiny brown nut, about 1 inch in diameter with a prominent scar at one side, whence the name, buckeye. One to three seeds are produced in each fruit, which is covered with coarse spines when young. The spines are lost in some species as the fruit wall becomes leathery and dry before splitting open, but are retained in others. These trees are all considered potentially dangerous to livestock, with some evidence that young growth, sprouts, and the mature nuts are especially dangerous. The nuts of horsechestnut have killed children, but they are unpleasant tasting and not usually consumed in the quantity necessary to produce symptoms. Apparently the poison in buckeyes is chemically related to the anticoagulant in sweetclover, but the disease is not similar to sweetclover poisoning. Buckeye poisoning is characterized principally by nervous symptoms.

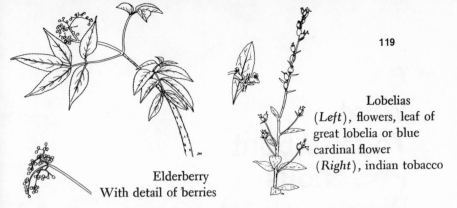

Lobelias
(*Left*), flowers, leaf of
great lobelia or blue
cardinal flower
(*Right*), indian tobacco

Elderberry
With detail of berries

Several supposed active compounds have been found in elderberry. Accidents involving children have occurred either from eating the roots or from using the pithy stems as blowguns. But the plant is only mildly poisonous and the fresh berries, the least toxic part, are essentially harmless. Uncooked berries may produce nausea if too many are eaten. Elderberry plants form coarse bushes as much as 12 feet tall, with soft, thick stems and conspicuous masses of purple-black or red berries when in fruit.

The common lobelias are erect, mostly unbranched, annual or perennial herbs. Some are weeds with relatively insignificant flowers while others, such as cardinal flower and blue cardinal flower, have showy inflorescences and are sometimes planted in gardens. A weedy species, Indian tobacco, received its common name from the early American settlers who observed that Indians smoked the dried leaves like tobacco. Experience showed that the species listed above all contained active substances, and soon they were used as medicinal plants to relieve a variety of ailments. Overdoses brought serious illness and sometimes death. Thus lobelias received their reputation as poisonous plants. The ability of primitive native populations to find and employ useful active compounds in plants is sometimes spectacular. The case of *Rauwolfia* and reserpine has already been described. The lobelias constitute another. The poisonous substance in the lobelias is an alkaloid, chemically and functionally similar to nicotine of tobacco.

Nicotine itself is a potent alkaloid. Small amounts absorbed into the blood stream can cause death. Commercially, nicotine is widely used as an insecticide. The amounts of nicotine contained in tobacco smoke are not highly poisonous. Nevertheless poisonous or lethal amounts can be obtained from cured smoking or chewing tobacco, from the foliage of field-grown tobacco, or from the foliage of the garden ornamental known as flowering tobacco or nicotiana.

6
What
To Do About
Poisonous
Plants

What is the antidote? The idea that each poison can be exactly countered in its effects by a particular medicine is an old one. For example, it was once believed that the poisonous effects of a scorpion bite could be cured by a preparation from aconite. Ben Jonson (1573-1637) wrote:

> I have heard that Aconite,
> Being timely taken, hath a healing might
> Against the scorpion's stroke; the proof we'll give
> That while two poisons wrestle we may live

"Antidotes" and directions for their use are found on the labels of household poisons. While the suggested remedies are valuable in case of accidental poisoning, they are usually not true antidotes in the strict or historical sense of the term because they do not inactivate the poisonous compound in a specific way. Instead they usually act to dilute the poison, absorb it so less will get into the blood stream, speed up the body's elimination of it, sooth the irritation it may cause, or produce vomiting to get rid of the poison in that manner. Acids to counteract alkalis and vice versa are more nearly antidotal in the historical meaning of the word. Poisonous substances from plants are rarely inactivated or neutralized by specific compounds. The United States Public Health Service says, "For all practical purposes, treatment of poisoning by plants is symptomatic and supportive; no generally accepted antidotal agents are available."

Treating symptoms is an art, not to be tried by the inexperienced. In acute poisoning it is usually desirable to induce vomiting as the quickest way to rid the body of the poisonous material. But in some

cases that invites complications more serious than the poisoning
it is supposed to remedy. This occurs for example when the poison
is a severely corrosive substance. The walls of the digestive tract
may be so badly burned by some plant poisons that they are weakened to the point where the spasmodic muscular contractions involved in vomiting might rupture them. A physician should make
the decision whether to induce vomiting or not.

In the rare case where a true antidotal agent is available, its use
is often tricky. Consider poisoning by cyanide for example. As we
have seen, cyanide, by combining with a vital enzyme, cytochrome,
in the body cells, prevents them from using the oxygen supplied
them by the blood stream. Cyanide, however, combines more easily
with reduced or chemically altered hemoglobin than it does with
cytochrome. The trick, then, is to convert enough blood hemoglobin to the reduced or altered form so that, as it circulates to all
parts of the body, it will pick up and remove the cyanide from the
body cells. This must be done quickly to prevent death. Minutes—
even seconds—count.

The quickest and easiest way to convert normal hemoglobin to
the reduced or altered form is to treat it with nitrite. Hemoglobin
reacts readily and quickly with nitrite injected into the blood stream
and is changed into reduced hemoglobin. While this flushes cyanide out of the body cells, it is unable to carry oxygen to them, and
this is the basis of nitrite poisoning. The physician, then, must convert to the reduced form enough hemoglobin to flush out sufficient
cyanide so that the cells may again use oxygen. At the same time
he must leave enough hemoglobin unconverted—hence still able to
carry oxygen—to provide the cells of the body with at least the
minimum amount necessary to support life.

Poisoning by nitrite can, in turn, be counteracted by chemicals
which act to reconvert reduced hemoglobin to the normal form
again. Methylene blue, commonly employed to do this, must be
administered promptly to be effective. Obviously, the whole business of treating cyanide or nitrite poisoning is touch and go, but
fortunately, the blood normally has reserves of oxygen-carrying
capacity far beyond its usual needs and also has mechanisms by
which cyanide and nitrites are rapidly excreted. The physician has
a real chance of success if he gets there quickly enough and has the
right medicines with him. Death in the average case of cyanide
poisoning or nitrite poisoning by plants doesn't take place for an
hour or more.

When a case of poisoning by plants is suspected, CALL YOUR PHYSI-
CIAN AND CALL HIM FAST! Better to be safe, even if embarrassed,
than dead.

Your physician can be expected to treat the symptoms in a case
of poisoning and take all warranted supportive measures. Usually
that is all he can do because no better measures are yet known.
Nevertheless he must check authoritative sources and be sure he
has taken all indicated measures in each case of plant poisoning.
To do this he needs to know what plant was involved. Physicians
cannot be expected to recognize each of the hundreds of poisonous
plants, let alone keep in their heads the details concerning poisonous compounds and the toxicities of each. What your physician
does know is how to find these details fast if you can tell him the
name of the plant—preferably the scientific name. It is your re-
sponsibility to know the names of the poisonous plants in your
yard or in the neighborhood where children play. The time saved
in identifying exactly a plant involved in a poisoning could be very
important.

Recognizing poisonous plants and learning their names is not as
difficult as might appear. Lots of aids are available to the person
willing to make a serious effort. This book with its illustrations will
help and there are some more technical works available. The agricultural colleges of many states have published bulletins describing
the common poisonous plants of their areas. If your state does not
have one, perhaps a neighboring state does. These bulletins can
usually be obtained free or at small expense at the county agent's
office or by writing the state college of agriculture or the state university.

The United States Department of Agriculture has some publica-
tions dealing with poisonous plants, principally of the West. A list
of these may be obtained from the Superintendent of Documents,
Washington, D.C. 20402.

The easiest way to learn to recognize a plant is to have it pointed
out for you. Usually, in almost every community one or more persons can be found who will help in a project to learn the local plants.
Such persons may be sought in the local high school, at the county
agent's office, or among horticulturists or garden-club members.

Physicians are now much better able to know what to do in a
case of poisoning than they were a few years ago because of the
establishment of poison-control centers in hospitals in major cities
throughout the country. Each center serves several functions. First,
it provides information to physicians twenty-four hours a day, seven

days a week, concerning the active ingredients and proper treatment of poisonings by thousands of potentially dangerous household items and natural substances. To meet this need, its files are constantly revised and kept up to date. Secondly, it serves as a focal point for the accumulation of information relating to poisonings which have occurred in its area.

A major reason why so little dependable information exists about the effect of poisonous plants on man is the lack of a centralized and regular method of reporting cases. Poison-control centers provide such a mechanism and the National Clearinghouse for Poison Control Centers, an arm of the United States Public Health Service, acts as a central repository for the accumulation, analysis, and dissemination of information collected by the centers across the country. Poison-control centers have also undertaken to function as educational centers for the prevention of poisonings and stand ready to warn the general population through radio and newspaper releases when situations presenting unusual poisoning hazards arise in their areas. Finally, most of them maintain a stock of materials and specialized instruments for the treatment of emergency poisonings. Usually these materials are maintained at the hospital where the center is located and it is expected that the poisoned patient will be brought there for treatment.

The best way to deal with the problem of poisonous plants is to avoid them. One rule always works: Never eat any part of any unknown plant. This rule has two corollaries. Eat only wholesome, properly prepared food products, and never use for medicinal purposes anything obtained directly from nature. If these common-sense regulations are followed, poisoning cannot occur. Allergenic reactions by contact with particular plants may still take place, but as explained earlier these are not true poisonings and rarely are they serious.

Nothing in this book need prevent anyone from enjoying the bounty of foods, flowers, and ornamentals which the world of plants offers. Properly prepared fruits and vegetables from the usual commercial and local sources, including the home garden, present no danger. One should not, of course, eat rhubarb blades or greened potato skins or sprouts. As for ornamentals, some, such as daphne, are really dangerous, particularly for children, but most, even though potentially poisonous, rarely cause actual trouble. Local conditions will determine whether it is dangerous to plant a particular ornamental or not. Usually there is little reason not to have such a plant if one wants it. Compare with the small number of cases of poisoning the large number of yews, rhododendrons, laurels, oleanders, and the like which are used in ornamental plantings. Chance of poisoning obviously is small, but it does exist, and such plants should not be chosen without knowledge of their possible toxicity.

Wild plants are another matter. The first impulse is to eradicate. With newer chemical herbicides available, this impulse is stronger than ever, but eradication is usually impractical, as we have seen in the case of halogeton, which spread from a few areas in Nevada in the early 1930's to more than 10 million acres in the Western states, by 1960. It seems unlikely that man will be able to limit its eventual spread into all areas to which it is adapted. But ranchers now know the danger in overgrazing ranges, since it opens the land to invasion by halogeton and other undesirable annual plants. They know which seasons are more dangerous than others; which stages of growth of the plant contain the most concentrated oxalate. They know the danger in taking hungry sheep into stands of halogeton and when they must take animals into dangerous range, they use preventive measures such as adding dicalcium phosphate to the diet and supplementary feeding of good alfalfa hay. Similar measures can be employed in dealing with other wild plants.

In summary, you can do these things about poisonous plants: First, learn the poisonous plants in your neighborhood. Know them by scientific name if possible. Second, take as a firm rule, and impress upon children, never to eat any unknown garden or wild plant, herb, shrub, or tree; never to make medical preparations from them. Also keep dangerous prunings, clippings, or garden cleanings away from livestock. Third, in any case of poisoning or suspected poisonings, call your physician, and be prepared, if at all possible, to tell him the name of the plant involved. Save evidence which might help identify the plant. Such evidence includes plant parts taken from the mouth or present in vomit or stools. Do not call the poison-control center yourself; the physician will do this. These centers are prepared to provide technical information to be used by a physician; for reasons of safety they are not prepared to suggest treatment unless a proper medical diagnosis has been made. If you cannot obtain a physician promptly, take the patient to the hospital.

As Pierre Joigneaux said,[5] exactly one hundred years ago: "We have to admit the existence of some absolutely bad plants, created perhaps solely to point out the merit of those plants that are useful to us, but these absolutely bad plants fortunately are quite rare."

[5] *Le Livre de la Ferme at des Maisons de Campagne.* Paris, France, 1865.

Index

Abrus, (Precatory bean Rosary Pea) 8, 25, 73, 82
Acetone, 50
Aconite (*Aconitum*), 109, 120
Aconitum, 109, 120
Acorns, 117
Aesculus, (Buckeye, Horsechestnut) 118
Agave, (Lechuguilla) 98
Agrostemma, (Corn cockle) 93
Aleurites, (tung tree) 93
Alfalfa, 87
Algae, 40, 45, 47
Alkali disease, 57
Alkaloids, 35, 65, 66, 69, 76, 77, 81, 109
Allergy, 16
Allium, (Onion) 24
Almond (*Prunus*) 24, 51, 88
Alocasis (*Alocasia*), 104
Amanita (*Amanita*), (Destroying angel, Fly agaric, Fly mushroom) 41, 43, 44, 45
Amaranth family, 87
Amaryllid family, 112
Amaryllis (*Amaryllis*), 113
Amines, toxic, 84
Amsinckia, (tarweed) 70
Amygdalin, 88
Anabaena, 46, 47
Anacardium, (cashew) 16
Anemia, 24
Anemonin, 90
Antibody, 26
Anticoagulant, 91
Antidotes, 120
Aphanizomenon, 46, 47
Apium, (Celery) 87
Apocynum, (Dogbane) 53
Apple (*Malus*), 24, 51
Apricot (*Prunus*), 24
Arisaema, (Jack-in-the-pulpit) 103
Arrow grass (*Triglochin*), 72
Artichoke, wild, 62
Arum family, 104
Asclepias, (Labriform milkweed) 50
Aspergillus, 54
Asphyxiation, 85, 89
Astragalus, (Loco, Loco weed, Poison vetch) 38, 56
Atropa, (Belladonna), 79
Autumn crocus (*Colchicum*), 111, 112
Avena, (Oat hay) 87

Bahia grass, 34
Baptisia (*Baptisia*), (False indigo) 110
Barley (*Hordeum*), 87
Barley, scabby (*Gibberella*), 70
Batyl alcohol, 84
Beans, lima (*Phaseolus*), 23
Beaver poison (*Cicuta*), 59
Beet (*Beta*), 24, 87, 103
Belladonna (drug), 21
Belladonna (*Atropa*), 79
Benzaldehyde, 88
Be-still-tree (*Thevetia*), 111
Beta, (Beet, Mangold) 24, 87, 103
Bighead, 95
Bird-of-paradise (*Poinciana*), 113
Bird seed, 105
Bitter almonds (*Prunus*), 88
Black locust (*Robinia*), 117
Bleeding disease, 90
Bleeding heart (*Dicentra*), 109
Blindness, 20, 74
Blind staggers, 57
Bloat, 69
Blood, 83
Blood clots, 91
Blood lily (*Haemanthus*), 113
Bloodroot (*Sanguinaria*), 82
Blowguns, poisonous, 119
Bluegreen algae, 45
Bone marrow, injury, 83
Bordeaux fungicide, 108
Botulism(*Clostridium*), 21, 25, 40, 73
Bouncing Bet (*Saponaria*), 92, 93
Box (*Buxus*), 114
Bracken fern (*Pteridium*), 82, 83
Brain, injury, 38
Brassica, (Cabbage, Mustard, Rape, Rutabaga, turnip) 22, 73, 87, 90
Brazil nut, 94
Bread poisoning, 80
Buckeye (*Aesculus*), 118
Buckwheat (*Fagopyrum*), 96
Bulb, poisonous, 112
Butter, poisonous, 50
Buttercup (*Ranunculus*), 89, 90
Buxus, (Box) 114

Cabbage (*Brassica*), 22
Cabbage family, 22
Cactus, candelabra (*Euphorbia*), 20
Caladium (*Caladium*, *Xanthosoma*), 104
Calcium, 24
Calcium deficiency, 103
Calcium oxalate, 99, 103
Calla, wild (*Calla*), 104
Caltha, (Cowslip) 90
Camas, 78
Cancer, 80
Candelabra cactus (*Euphorbia*), 20
Cannabis, (Hemp Marihuana) 69, 104, 105
Caper Spurge (*Euphorbia*), 19
Cardinal flower (*Lobelia*), 119
Cardioactive glycosides, 111, 112
Carolina jessamine (*Gelsemium*), 113
Carotte à moreau (*Cicuta*), 59
Carrot family, 59, 63
Carrot, wild, 62
Cashew (*Anacardium*), 16
Cassava (*Manihot*), 73
Castor bean (*Ricinus*), 7, 72, 73
Castor oil, 73
Celandine poppy (*Chelidonium*), 82
Celery (*Apium*), 87
Cercocarpus, (Mountain mahogany) 51
Chelidonium, (Celandine poppy) 82
Cherry (*Prunus*), 24
Cherry, wild (*Prunus*), 24, 51, 88
Chlorophyll, 96
Choking, 47
Christmas rose (*Helleborus*), 109
Cicuta (Beaver poison, Carotte à moreau, Cowbane, False parsley, Fever root, Water hemlock, Mockeel root, Muskrat weed, Musquash root, Snakeroot, Snakeweed, Spotted cowbane, Spotted hemlock, Spotted parsley), 58, 71
Cinquefoil, sulphur, 105
Citric acid, 101
Clams, poisonous, 46
Claviceps, (Ergot) 34, 73

Climbing lily (*Gloriosa*), 112
Climbing nightshade (*Solanum*), 75
Clostridium, (Botulism) 21, 25, 40, 73
Coat color, 108
Cocklebur (*Xanthium*), 66, 67
Colchicine, 112
Colchicum, (Autumn crocus) 112
Colocasia, (Elephant's ear) 104
Columbus grass (*Sorghum*), 55
Common names, 28
Composite family, 87
Conium, (Poison hemlock) 62
Control of poisoning, 101, 122
Control of poisonous plants, 124
Convallaria, (Lily-of-the-valley) 111
Convulsions, 35, 61, 73, 85
Copper, 108
Corn (*Zea*), 87
Corn cockle (*Agrostemma*), 92, 93
Corn, molded, 54, 170
Coughing, 47
Coumarin, 91
Cowbane (*Cicuta*), 59
Cow cockle (*Saponaria*), 93
Cowslip (*Caltha*), 90
Crabs, poisonous, 46
Crinum lily (*Crinum*), 113
Crotalaria (*Crotalaria*), 79, 80
Crown-of-thorns (*Euphorbia*), 20
Cyanide, 23, 24, 54, 72, 73, 88, 115, 121
Cyanogenetic glycosides, 51
Cyclopia, 77
Cypress spurge (*Euphorbia*), 20
Cytochrome, 121

2, 4-D, 87
Daffodil (*Narcissus*), 112
Dallis grass, 34
Daphne (*Daphne*), 36, 37, 123
Datura, (thornapple), 79
Deadly amanita (*Amanita*), 41, 44, 45
Death camas (*Zigadenus*), 76, 78
Death's cup, 43
Delphinium, (Larkspur) 68, 70, 109
Dermatitis, 16
Destroying angel (*Amanita*), 41
Dicentra, (Bleeding heart, Dutchman's breeches, Squirrel corn) 109
Dicoumarin, 91
Dieffenbachia, (Dumbcane) 103
Digitalis (drug), 21, 88

Digitalis (*Digitalis*), (Foxglove) 88, 111
Dinoflagellates, 46
Dioscorides, 31
Dogbane (*Apocynum*), 53, 54
Dogbane family, 53, 54, 111
Dumbcane (*Dieffenbachia*), 103, 104
Dutchman's breeches (*Dicentra*), 109, 110
Dynamite poisoning, 86

Edema, 94
Elderberry (*Sambucus*), 119
Elephant's ear (*Colocasia*), 104
Embryo poison, 78
Emphysema, 74
English yew (*Taxus*), 65
Enzyme, poisonous, 82
Equisetum, (Horsetail) 82
Ergot, (*Claviceps*), 34, 35, 73
Ergot alkaloids, 35
Estrogen, 71
Eupatorium, (Snakeroot, White snakeroot) 48
Euphorbia, (Candelabra cactus, Crown of thorns, Pencil tree, Poinsettia, Snow-on-the-Mountain, Spurges, 8, 19, 20, 25, 90

Fagopyrum, (Buckwheat), 96
False hellebore (*Veratrum*), 76, 77
False indigo (*Baptisia*), 110
False morel (*Gyromitra*), 42
False parsley (*Cicuta*), 59
Female hormone, 71
Fern, bracken (*Pteridium*), 82
Fern, jimmy (*Notholaena*), 54
Fever root (*Cicuta*), 59
Fish, poisoned, 47
Flowering tobacco (*Nicotiana*), 119
Fly agaris, fly mushroom (*Amanita*), 41, 43, 44
Food poisoning, 40
Food, spoiled, 40
Foxglove (*Digitalis*), 87, 88
Fritillaria (*Fritillaria*), 112
Frog spit, 45
Fungi, 40

Galanthus, (Snowdrop), 113
Galerina, (*Galerina*), 42
Gangrene, 34, 73
Garget (*Phytolacca*), 116
Gas, poisonous, 86
Gelsemium, (Carolina jessamine, Jessamine yellow Jessamine) 113
Genus, 29
Gibberella, (Scabby barley) 70

Gloriosa, (Climbing lily, Glory lily) 112
Glory lily (*Gloriosa*), 112
Glycosides, 87
Goiter, 22, 90
Gonyaulax, 46
Goosefoot family, 87
Grain, molded, 70
Grain, poisonous, 93
Grape, 116
Grass, Argentine bahia, 34
Grass, Dallis, 34
Greasewood (*Sarcobatus*), 100
Ground hemlock (*Taxus*), 62, 65
Groundsell (*Senecio*), 80
Gymnodinium, 47
Gyromitra (False morel) 42

HCN. *See* cyanide
Haemanthus, (Blood lily) 113
Hallucination, 106
Halogeton (*Halogeton*), 100, 124
Hay fever, 16
Hay, oat (*Avena*), 87
Heath family, 51, 104
Hedge, 114
Hellebore, false (*Veratrum*), 76
Hellebore (*Helleborus*), 109
Helleborus, (Christmas rose) 109
Hemlock, 62
Hemlock, ground (*Taxus*), 62, 65
Hemlock, poison (*Conium*), 62
Hemlock, water (*Cicuta*), 58, 71
Hemoglobin, 121
Hemorrhage, 74, 83, 91
Hemp (*Cannabis*), 105
Herbals, 32
Hippomane, (Manchineel) 19
Homeopathic medicine, 71
Hoof, deformity, 57
Honey, poisonous, 113
Hordeum, (Barley) 87
Hormone, female, 71
Horsebrush (*Tetradymia*), 98, 99
Horsechestnut, (*Aesculus*), 118
Horsenettle (*Solanum*), 74
Horsetail (*Equisetum*), 82, 83
Hyacinth (*Hyacinthus*), 112
Hyacinthus, 112
Hydrangea (*Hydrangea*), 114
Hydroquinone, 67
Hypericum, (St. Johnswort) 96

Indian tobacco (*Lobelia*), 119
Insanity, 79
Iodine, 22

Ipomoea, (Sweet potato) 87
Iris (*Iris*), 113, 114

Jack-in-the-pulpit (*Arisaema*), 102, 103
Japanese yew (*Taxus*), 62, 65
Jaundice, 44
Jessamine (*Gelsemium*), 113
Jewelry, poisonous, 27
Jimmy fern (*Notholaena*), 54, 55
Jimsonweed. See thornapple
Johnson grass (*Sorghum*), 55, 56
Jonquil (*Narcissus*), 113

Kalmia, (Laurel, Mountain laurel) 51, 124
Kidney injury, 75, 99, 117

Labels, warning, 25
Labrador tea (*Ledum*), 51
Labriform milkweed (*Asclepias*), 50, 51
Lacquer, 16
Lactic acid, 86
Lameness, 57
Lantana (*Lantana*), 98
Larkspur (*Delphinium*), 68, 69, 70, 109
Lathyrus, (Sweet pea) 85
Laurel (*Kalmia*), 124
Laurel, mountain (*Kalmia*), 51
Leafy spurge (*Euphorbia*), 19
Lechuguilla (*Agave*), 98
Ledum, (Labrador tea) 51
Legumes, legume family, 40, 108
Leucothoe, (Sierra laurel) 51
Ligustrum, (Privet) 114
Lily, blood (*Haemanthus*), 113
Lily, climbing (*Gloriosa*), 112
Lily, crinum (*Crinum*), 113
Lily family, 112
Lily, glory (*Gloriosa*), 112
Lily-of-the-valley (*Convallaria*), 110, 111
Lima bean (*Phaseolus*), 23
Liver injury, 44, 70, 74, 76, 80, 96
Lobelia (*Lobelia*), (Cardinal Flower, Indian tobacco) 119
Loco, locoweed (*Astragalus, Oxytropis*), 38, 39
Lung injury, 86
Lupine (*Lupinus*), 110
Lupinus, 110
Lycopersicon, (tomato) 22

Malic acid, 101
Malus, (apple) 24, 51
Manchineel (*Hippomane*), 19, 20
Mangold (*Beta*), 87

Manihot, (Cassava, tapioca) 73
Marihuana (*Cannabis*), 69, 104, 107
Mayapple (*Podophyllum*), 115
Meat, poisonous, 53
Medicago, 87
Melilotus, (Sweetclover) 90, 118
Menispermum, (Moonseed) 116
Menziesia, (Rusty leaf) 51
Methylene blue, 121
Microcystis, 46, 47
Milk, poisonous, 48
Milk, sickness, 48
Milkweed (*Asclepias*), 50
Milkweed family, 53
Mistletoe, American (*Phoradendron*), 84
Mistletoe, European (*Viscum*), 84
Mock-eel root (*Cicuta*), 59
Mold, 54, 70
Molded grain, 70
Mollusks, poisonous, 46
Molybdenum, 107
Monkey-face lambs, 77
Moonseed (*Menispermum*), 115, 116
Morel, 42
Morel, false (*Gyromitra*), 42
Morphine, 21
Moss, 40, 45
Mountain laurel (*Kalmia*), 51, 52
Mountain mahogany (*Cercocarpus*), 51
Mushroom, 41, 42, 43, 44
Muskrat weed (*Cicuta*), 59
Musquash root (*Cicuta*), 59
Mustard (*Brassica*), 87, 90
Mustard family, 87, 90
Mustard oils, 90

Names, common, 28
Names, scientific, 29
Narcissus (*Narcissus*), (Daffodil, Jonquil), 112
Narcotic, 105
Nectar, poisonous, 79
Nerine (*Nerine*), 113
Nerium, (Oleander) 8, 53, 124
Nervous system, injury, 76
Nettle horse (*Solanum*), 75
Nicotiana (*Nicotiana*), (Flowering tobacco, tobacco) 119
Nicotine, 65, 119
Nightshade family, 87
Nightshades (*Solanum*), 22, 23, 75
Nitrate, 72, 73, 74, 85
Nitrite, 121
Nitro-cellulose, 86
Nitrogen gas, 86
Nolina, (Sacahuiste) 98
Notholaena, (Jimmy fern) 54
Nuts, poisonous, 111, 118

Oak (*Quercus*), 116, 117
Oat hay (*Avena*), 87
Oenanthe (*Oenanthe*), 61
Oleander (*Nerium*), 8, 53, 124
Onion (*Allium*), 24
Opium, 81, 82, 105
Opium poppy (*Papaver*), 81
Orfila, 37
Oriental poppy (*Papaver*), 81
Ornithogalum, (Star-of-Bethlehem) 112
Oxalates, oxalic acid, 24, 99, 101
Oxytropis, (Loco, locoweed) 38
Oysters, poisonous, 46

Papaver, (Opium poppy, Oriental poppy, poppy) 81, 109
Paralysis, 38, 46, 65, 69, 85
Peach (*Prunus*), 24, 51, 88
Pencil tree (*Euphorbia*), 20
Phaseolus, (Lima beans) 23
Philodendron (*Philodendron*), 104
Phoradendron, (American Mistletoe) 84
Photosensitization, 71, 74, 94
Phylloerythrin, 96
Phytolacca. (Garget, Pigeonberry, Pokeweed, Scoke) 116
Phytotoxin, 25, 73, 82
Pieris (*Pieris*), 51
Pigeonberry (*Phytolacca*), 116
Plankton, 45
Podophyllum (Mayapple), 115
Poinciana (*Poinciana*), (Bird-of-Paradise), 113
Poinsettia (*Euphorbia*), 8, 20, 21, 25
Poison Control Centers, 122
Poison hemlock (*Conium*), 59, 62, 63
Poison ivy (*Toxicodendron*), 16, 17
Poison oak (*Toxicodendron*), 16
Poison sumac (*Toxicodendron*), 16, 18, 19
Poison vetch (*Astragalus*), 56
Pokeweed (*Phytolacca*), 116
Pond scum, 45
Poppy (*Papaver*), 81, 82, 109
Pore fungi, 42
Portulaca, (Purslane) 103
Potato (*Solanum*), 123
Precatory bean (*Abrus*), 8, 25, 26, 73, 82
Privet (*Ligustrum*), 114
Proteins, poisonous, 82
Protoanemonin, 90

Prunus, (Almond, Apricot, Bitter almonds, Cherry, Wild Cherry, Peach) 24, 51, 88
Prussic acid—see cyanide
Pteridium, (Bracken fern) 82
Pulmonary emphysema, 74
Puncture vine (*Tribulus*), 98
Purslane (*Portulaca*), 103

Queen Anne's lace, 59, 62
Quercus, (Oak) 117

Radiation poisoning, 83
Ranunculin, 90
Ranunculus, (Buttercup) 90
Rape (*Brassica*), 73, 74, 87
Rash, skin, 16
Rat poison, 90
Rauwolfia (*Rauwolfia*), 30, 119
Red squill (*Urginea*), 112
Red tides, 47
Reserpine, 30, 119
Resinoid, 104, 115
Rheum, (Rhubarb) 101, 123
Rhododendron (*Rhododendron*), 51 124
Rhubarb (*Rheum*), 123
Ricinus, (Castor bean) 7, 73
Robinia, (Black locust, locust) 117
Root, poisonous, 60
Rosary pea (*Abrus*), 8, 25
Rose family, 40, 51, 88
Rumen, 69
Rumex (Sorrell), 103
Russian thistle (*Salsola*), 103
Rusts, 41, 45
Rustyleaf (*Menziesia*), 51
Rutabaga (*Brassica*), 22

Sacahuiste (*Nolina*), 97, 98
Salsola, (Russian thistle) 103
Sambucus, (Elderberry) 119
Sanguinaria, (Bloodroot) 82
Sap, burning, 19
Saponaria, (Bouncing Bet, Cow cockle) 93
Saponins, 92
Sarcobatus, (Greasewood) 100
Scabby barley, 70
Scientific names, 29
Scilla, (Squill) 112
Scoke (*Phytolacca*), 116
Screenings, poisonous, 70, 93
Seaweed, 45
Seed, poisonous, 7, 8, 25, 67, 68, 79, 93, 118
Selenium, 55, 107
Senecio (Groundsel), 80
Shellfish poisoning, 46, 70
Sierra laurel (*Leucothoe*), 51
Silage, 86

Silo-filler's disease, 86
Simples, 33
Skeletal deformity, 85
Skewer, poisonous, 53
Skunk cabbage (*Symplocarpus*), 102, 104
Sleep, horses, 58
Sleepy grass (*Stipa*), 57, 58, 70
Smuts, 41, 45
Snakeroot (*Cicuta*), 59
Snakeroot (*Eupatorium*), 48
Snake venom, 26
Snakeweed (*Cicuta*), 59
Snowdrop (*Galanthus*), 113
Snow-on-the-mountain (*Euphorbia*), 19, 20
Socrates, 64
Solanine, 22, 75
Solanum (Climbing nightshade, Horsenettle, Nightshades, Potato), 22, 75, 123
Sorghum (*Sorghum*), (Columbus grass, Johnson grass, Sorgrass, Sudan grass), 54, 55, 72, 73, 87
Sorgrass (*Sorghum*), 55
Sorrel (*Rumex*), 103
Spinach (*Spinacia*), 24, 103
Spinacia, 24, 103
Spoiled food, 40
Spotted cowbane (*Cicuta*), 50
Spotted hemlock (*Cicuta*), 59
Spotted parsley (*Cicuta*), 59
Spotted spurge (*Euphorbia*), 19
Spurges (*Euphorbia*), 19, 90
Squill (*Scilla*), 112
Squirrel corn (*Dicentra*), 109
St. Johnswort (*Hypericum*), 96
Stachybotrys, 54
Staggers, 57
Star-of-Bethlehem (*Ornithogalum*), 112
Stipa (Sleepy grass), 58, 70
Succession powders, 31
Sudan grass (*Sorghum*), 54, 55, 72, 73, 87
Sulfur, 107
Sulfur cinquefoil, 105
Sumac, poison (*Toxicodendron*), 16, 19
Sunburn, 71, 94
Sun spurge (*Euphorbia*), 19
Sweetclover (*Melilotus*), 90, 118
Sweet pea (*Lathyrus*), 85
Sweet potato (*Ipomoea*), 87
Symplocarpus, (Skunk cabbage), 104

Tapioca (*Manihot*), 73
Tarweed (*Amsinckia*), 70
Taxus (English yew, Ground hemlock, Japanese yew, Yew), 62, 65
Teartness, 107
Temperature, elevated, 83
Tetradymia, (Horsebrush), 98

Thalidomide, 77
Thevetia, (Be-still-tree, Yellow oleander), 111
Thiaminase, 82
Thiamine, 82
Thiooxazolidone, 22
Thirst, 79
Thornapple (*Datura*), 78, 79
Thyroid, 22
Toadstool, 41
Tobacco (*Nicotiana*), 119
Tomato (*Lycopersicon*), 22
Tongue, swelling, 103
Toxicodendron, (Poison ivy, Poison oak, Poison sumac), 16, 19
Tranquilizers, 30
Treatment, 120
Trembles, 48
Tremetol, 50
Tribulus (Puncture vine), 98
Triglochin, (Arrow grass), 72
Tung tree (*Aleurites*), 93
Turnip (*Brassica*), 22, 87

Uranium, 56
Uremic poisoning, 99
Urginea, (Red squill), 112

Venom, snake, 26
Veratrum, (False hellebore), 76
Vetch, poison (*Astragalus*), 56
Viscum (European Mistletoe), 84
Vision, disturbed, 79
Vitamin B1, 82
Vomiting, 71

Warfarin, 92
Water hemlock (*Cicuta*), 58, 59, 71
Water, poisonous, 46
Wheat, 70, 87
White blood cells, 83
White Snakeroot (*Eupatorium*), 48
Wild animals, poisoned, 46
Wild artichoke, 62
Wild calla (*Calla*), 104
Wild carrot, 59, 62
Wild cherry (*Prunus*), 24, 51, 88
Wild parsnip, 59, 62
Wisteria (*Wisteria*), 15, 16, 114

Xanthium (Cocklebur), 67
Xanthosoma, (Caladium), 104

Yellow jessamine (*Gelsemium*), 113
Yellow oleander (*Thevetia*), 111
Yew (*Taxus*), 62, 65, 114, 124

Zea, 54, 87, 170
Zigadenus, (Death camus), 76, 78